THE DEMING ROUTE

TO

QUALITY AND PRODUCTIVITY

Road Maps and Roadblocks

THE DEMING ROUTE
TO
QUALITY AND PRODUCTIVITY

Road Maps and Roadblocks

by
William W. Scherkenbach

CEE PRESS
BOOKS
WASHINGTON, D.C.

ASQC
QUALITY PRESS
MILWAUKEE, WI.

CEEPress Books, George Washington
University, Washington, D.C. 20052
1st Printing, May, 1986
2nd Printing, September, 1986
3rd Printing, February, 1987
4th Printing, May, 1987
5th Printing, October, 1987

THE DEMING ROUTE
TO
QUALITY AND PRODUCTIVITY

Road Maps and Roadblocks

Executive Editor
"J" "W" Perkins, Director
Continuing Engineering Education Program
George Washington University
Washington, D.C. 20052

Printed in U.S.A. and distributed world-wide by
Mercury Press/Fairchild Publications
Rockville, MD 20852, (301) 770-6177
ISBN:0941893-00-6
Library of Congress Catalog Card No. 87-401099

MERCURYPRESS

12230 Wilkins Avenue
Rockville, Maryland 20852

TABLE OF CONTENTS

FOREWORD

Mr. Scherkenbach's invitation to me to write a foreword to his book gives me unusual satisfaction. First, this book will supplement and enhance my own works and my teaching. His masterful understanding of a system, of a process, of a stable system and of an unstable system, are obvious and effective in his work as well as in his teaching.

Mr. Scherkenbach exposes in a masterful way the inadequacy of zero defects. It is no longer sufficient just to meet specifications, no longer sufficient to have the customer not complain. It is necessary, for good business, to have customers that boast about your product or service, stay with you, and bring in a friend for new business.

I cannot refrain from feeling satisfaction that Mr. Scherkenbach took all my courses at the Graduate School of Business Administration of New York University over a period of years, and that I have had the pleasure to work with him and to learn from him in the Ford Motor Company.

W. Edwards Deming
Washington
May 1986

INTRODUCTION

I must state from the very start that reading this book is absolutely no substitute for reading Dr. Deming's book *Out of the Crisis* or its predecessor, *Quality, Productivity and Competitive Position*. My only hope is to help people improve their understanding of Dr. Deming's all-important message. This book is a collection of my observations, ideas, and interpretations of a philosophy formed and practiced by an "apprentice statistician".

It is easy for me to say that the theory covered in this book applies to all processes and disciplines. But if you the reader do not identify with the theory enough to understand it and to look deeper into it, then this might be a very correct book, but of little use. How will I persuade you to listen to the theory? Through gossip (case studies for you business school graduates). Now, this is not the common ordinary gossip of the "if the shoe fits, wear it" variety. The intent of this gossip is to persuade you to understand that you can apply the theory to your everyday work.

This book presents Dr. Deming's Fourteen Points in the order that makes logical sense to me. I do this so that you might better understand the philosophy as I unfold it. You must understand that the one-sentence descriptions of the Fourteen Points are constantly being improved by Dr. Deming. The Fourteen Points themselves, however, are not changing. No one sentence or even chapter can really capture the full intent of one point. It takes reading and rereading and pondering and doing to understand his philosophy. There is no instant pudding. Some chapters are more developed than others. This is because my understanding of Dr. Deming's Fourteen Points is more developed for some than for others. Additionally, because this book is meant to supplement Dr. Deming's book, some chapters are shorter than others because I don't have any more to add.

I was deeply honored when Dr. Deming asked me to write this book about his Fourteen Points. Ever since I first studied under him at the New York University Graduate School of Business in 1972, I have worked to help him become known for turning America around, not just Japan. But America cannot be turned around unless you, the reader, turn around. It won't be easy. Change never is. But it can be done. You must not wait for your boss, your government, your industry, your company, or your university. The change begins right now, with you.

Like Dr. Deming, I have had the opportunity to work only with great people. I particularly wish to note a group of people who have contributed immeasurably to the understanding and implementation of Dr. Deming's philosophy in industry. They are my associates at Ford Motor Company: Ed Baker, Peter Jessup, Narendra Sheth, Victor Kane, Scott Rezabek, Harry Artinian, Gerd Blümel, and Bill Craft. Each separately and together have learned from and improved on the teachings of Dr. Deming. Their work is reflected in this book. Other masters who have helped my understanding include Dave Chambers and Ron Moen. Three people in top management were particularly influential in learning and applying Dr. Deming's philosophy: Jim Bakken, Bill Conway, and Don Petersen. I have had the privilege of learning from and arguing with each of them.

But above all is Dr. Deming. It was he who was the initiator of this book. It was he who reviewed and improved my manuscript innumerable times. It was him.

W. W. S.
Northville
3 November 1985

Chapter 1

Create constancy of purpose toward improvement of product and service, with the aim to become competitive, stay in business, and provide jobs. (Point 1)

The business process starts with the customer. In fact, if it is not started with the customer, it all too many times abruptly ends with the customer. Dr. Deming has said for decades that the customer is the most important part of the production line.

> Consumer research is an integral part of production...Without consumer research, the product has little chance of being maximally useful, or made in the most economical quantities. In fact, a manufacturing concern can hardly hope to stay in business today without vigorous consumer research.[1]

> It is a mistake to suppose that efficient production of product and service can, with certainty, keep an organization solvent and ahead of its competition. It is possible and, in fact, fairly easy for an organization to go downhill and out of business making the wrong product or offering the wrong type of service, even though everyone in the organization performs with devotion, employing statistical methods and every other aid that can boost efficiency.[2]

One of the first things Dr. Deming taught the Japanese in the late 1940s was how to conduct a survey. He taught them that before they asked him to come back in 1950 to talk about other methods of quality management.

> In the olden days, before the industrial era, the tailor, the carpenter, the shoemaker, the milkman, the blacksmith knew his customers by name. He knew whether they were satisfied, and what he should do to improve appreciation for his product. With the expansion of industry, this personal touch was lost. The wholesaler, the jobber, and the retailer have now stepped in, and in effect have set up a barrier between the manufacturer and the ultimate consumer. But sampling, a new science, steps in and pierces that barrier...

> Manufacturers used to think of manufacturing in three steps: Design it, Make it, and Try to sell it. These three steps were thought of as completely independent.

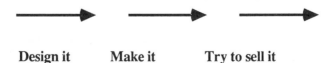

Design it   **Make it**   **Try to sell it**

Figure 1-1

In the new way, management introduces, through consumer research, a fourth step, and runs through the four steps in a cycle, over and over as in Figure 1-2, and not in the line of Figure 1-1.

1. Design the product (with appropriate tests).

2. Make it, test it in the production line and in the laboratory.

3. Put it on the market.

4. Test it in service. Through market research, find out what the user thinks of it, and why the non-user has not bought it.

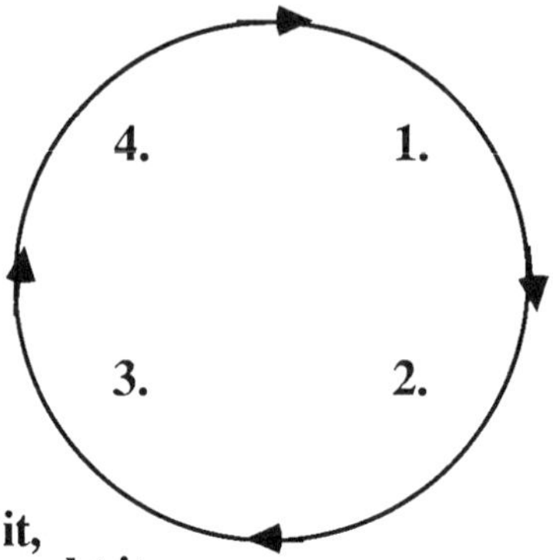

Figure 1-2

This fourth step was impossible until recently—i.e., it could not be carried out economically or reliably. Modern statistical techniques, such as sampling and design of experiment, combined with the arts of questioning and interviewing, provide information on consumer reactions with economy and reliability.

The fourth step, communication between the manufacturer and the user and the potential user, gives the public a chance. It gives the user a better product, better suited to his needs and cheaper. Democracy in industry, one might say.

Consumer research is a continuous process by which the product is continually improved and modified to meet changing requirements of the consumer. Consumer research, intelligently used, enables the manufacturer to run his factory on an even keel, neither greatly over-producing nor under-producing. He does not let out 300 men one month and try to recover them the next.[1]

It is this customer-driven, team-fueled, and even-keel approach to business that forms the basis for the constancy that Dr. Deming is urging. But until recently, the customer has been the forgotten half of the equation. Management has often focused attention inward to get engineering and manufacturing to learn about each other's problems and to work together as a team. This is an improvement that will pay great dividends. But of equal importance is the teamwork between marketing and sales and product planning and engineering. Marketing and sales people must determine the customers' needs and then pass this usable information on to design and engineering for translation into something that can be produced. One of the bigger problems in this process is to define operationally the customers' needs throughout the organization. (I strongly suggest that you read Chapter 9 of Dr. Deming's book *Out of the Crisis* to get a better understanding of operational definitions.) Those needs must be communicable to all concerned with the same understanding of the term "needs" today as yesterday. A requirement that a steel plate be "free from rust" has no meaning unless a specific method is given to determine just how much rust is on a steel plate. For example, is the test based on an electron microscope examination or just an eyeball not seeing any rust? Additionally, the answer must be unambiguous. A requirement that an engineering drawing must be "on time" has no meaning unless it is operationally defined. If the drawing is only a few minutes late, is it on time? How about if it is early? What if it is on time but not complete? (This is a situation which often occurs with fixed milestones and little time or resources to meet them.) Because of fear in the organization, the visible deadline is not missed, but the quality of work delivered is compromised, knowing full well that a change order will be processed later to make it "right."

We literally cannot be competitive in international markets unless we can operationally define our customers' needs. In order to meet those needs and expectations at a price they are willing to pay, we must first know them.

Some manufacturers think of consumer research (or market research) as analysis of complaints from purchasers and users...But complaints come from a very biased sample of consumers. Complaints do not provide communication with the other consumers nor with the nonconsumer.[1]

Only top management can establish the constancy of purpose necessary to know and then meet the customers' needs and expectations. Only they can make policy, establish the set of core values, or set the long-term course for the corporation. Many companies do have policy statements that reflect top management's visions (some might say hallucinations). But it is easy for the folks on the top floor to get religion. Talk is cheap. Top management might be able to set the course, but may never realize that it is also their responsibility to provide a roadmap so that the rest of the organization may follow. For some members of management, getting their people to follow is easy. They apply a definition of leadership which states "Find a parade and walk in front of it." Others in top management will say that this call for constancy of purpose is obvious. They plan for the long term and do care about the future.

> Are chief executive officers concerned only with short-term results? No, that's just a popular myth. So concludes a study by Harvard Business School of 45 ranking executives of major industrial firms. Surveyors interviewed the business leaders. They also studied confidential financial and planning documents

of their corporations. A finding: Main aim of top managers is not to maximize shareholder wealth. It is "the survival of the corporation in which they have invested so much of themselves psychologically and professionally."₃

However, as much as many companies do have long-range plans (i.e., 5-year plans and 10-year plans) those visions and management intentions are thwarted by systems, styles, and operating precedents (We do a lot of things because we have always done them that way. You won't find it in writing.) which force decisions and initiative to focus on the short term rather than on the hoped-for long term.

Many executives have told me that there is a very good reason why a lot of decisions are made that focus on short-term results. They say that if they don't make it to the next week or the next month or the next quarter, there won't be a future to plan for. This might have been a reasonable approach when we, as Western businessmen, were only competing against each other. We were all essentially managing by the same rules. Those rules were established in great part by the economist John Keynes. Peter Drucker observed:

> Keynes is in large measure responsible for the extreme short-term focus of modern politics, of modern economics and modern business—the short-term focus that is now, with considerable justice, considered a major weakness of American policymakers, both in government and in business...today's short-term measures have long-term impacts. They irrevocably make the future. Not to think through the futurity of short-term decisions and their impact long after "we are all dead" is irresponsible.₄

Keynes died in 1946. But close to forty years later, institutional money managers are exerting Keynesian pressures on business.

> Within minutes of ITT Corp.'s announcement on July 11 that it was cutting its dividend by nearly two-thirds so it could afford heavy investments in the U.S. telecommunications business, money managers stampeded to dump their shares...The money manager's power acts as a Damoclean sword over companies today, forcing chief executives to keep earnings on a consistently upward track, quarter by quarter, even if it means frustrating their long-range plans.₅

In spite of this long period of short-term pressures, we are now in a new economic age. We are now competing against businessmen who are not playing by the same rules we are. They are not compromising the future to the extent that we have been. And as the future has a tendency to creep up on us before we know it, Western executives should keep this in mind when they make decisions. There certainly will be trade-offs between the problems of today and the opportunities of tomorrow. Just don't foreclose on the future to the degree that you have been doing. One of the secrets for allocation of resources for the future is the ability of an organization or group of organizations to balance teamwork and competition.[6] They do not have to be mutually exclusive. In order for this to be true, William Ouchi observes that "Social Memory" must exist. Without it, no one would be willing to step aside now for someone else, or to give up short-term gains, or to give up the proverbial bird in the hand.

> The incentive is that all parties know that their sacrifice today will be remembered and repaid in the future. No one has to depend solely upon the beneficiary of his or her cooperation to remember and repay; the memory is firmly and reliably lodged in several units of social memory, and repayment or retribution is a certainty.[7]

Constancy of purpose affects the opportunities of tomorrow. But the course needs to be set today. Establishing constancy of purpose is a problem of the mean or central tendency. It is certainly a necessary condition for business success. But it is not sufficient. The wishes and hopes of top management for the future might be very noble, and in fact be on a course that could effectively meet customer needs and expectations except for one thing: the rest of the company is off somewhere else doing their best. As Dr. Deming says, "Do you know that doing your best is not good enough? You have to know what to do. Then do your best." These are profound words because they summarize the two important messages in this first point: that of knowing what to do—establishing the constancy of purpose and then doing your best—maintaining consistency of purpose.

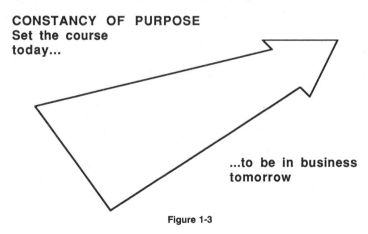

CONSTANCY OF PURPOSE
Set the course
today...

...to be in business
tomorrow

Figure 1-3

Maintaining consistency of purpose is a problem of the range or dispersion. It is a problem of today which directly affects the opportunities of tomorrow. Even if the aim is focused on the center of the target, if the rest of the company doesn't follow the course, if everyone is off doing his best without knowing what to do, the results will not live up to management's expectations. The problem of managing the spread or dispersion is often-times much more difficult than managing the mean. It is this reality that heavily contributes to the inefficiencies of Western business.

CONSISTENCY OF PURPOSE
Strives to reduce
the spread...

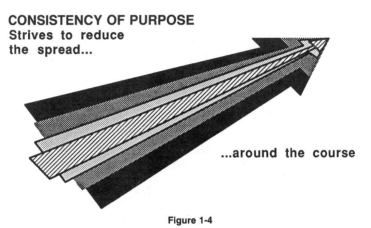

...around the course

Figure 1-4

Management does not understand that the world is filled with variability. They in fact "know" just the opposite, that the world is deterministic. They "know" that:
- All of the columns and rows must add up exactly.
- Two is less than three.
- All variances should be explained.
- Everyone should "do it right the first time."
- If you improve quality, quantity will correspondingly drop.

What they don't know, as Dr. Deming says, is what questions to ask. Management by walking around (MBWA) will be of little use if one doesn't even know what questions to ask. The remainder of this book, and, in fact, the whole of Dr. Deming's philosophy, is directed to knowing what questions to ask. And as the great economist, Joseph A. Schumpeter felt, the questions are always more important than the answers.[8]

Chapter 2

Adopt the new philosophy. We are in a new economic age, created by Japan. Western management must awaken to the challenge, must learn their responsibilities, and take on leadership for change. (Point 2)

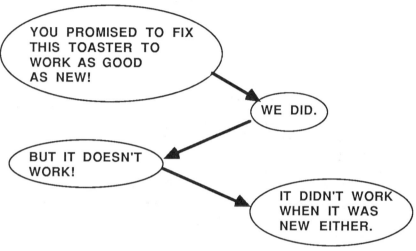

Figure 2-1

Adopt the new philosophy. Why? What's wrong with the old philosophy? Didn't it turn us into a great industrial society? Many people think that all we really need to do is get back to the basics of business and everything will be okay. What does management "know" about the basics of business? Well, read this excerpt from an excellent article by Myron Tribus.

Consider a trucking firm managed by a man educated according to current management methods taught in American schools of business management. He will consider it his job to run the company as profitably as he can and to expand its business. To do so, he may call upon the best consultants he can get to help him design the best possible systems for dispatch, routing and maintenance. He may set up work standards for the drivers and institute computer-based procedures to keep track of the performance of the drivers, trucks and dispatchers. He will institute the best methods of dispatching he can devise, either on his own or as gleaned from trade magazines or meetings of his association. He will study his markets and their opportunities. He will keep extensive records of income and expense, ever on the alert for opportunities to increase his profit.

Of course, he will not be able to manage his empire alone. As the organization grows, he will institute methods to see that his desires for efficiency and performance are carried out. Perhaps he will adopt "management by objectives" and teach the methods to those who report directly to him and to others. He may assign as much as five percent of his workforce to data gathering and performance evaluation, helping him to search for possible profit opportunities.

He may hire outside lecturers to give "motivation" lectures to his workers. He asks his division managers to nominate a "driver of the month" who will be suitably recognized and rewarded for superior performance.

He identifies poor performers and either gives them additional education and training or replaces them. He may even have his own driver education school or hire the use of one to be sure his drivers know how to do their jobs effectively.

He may hire outside evaluators to make visits to his customers to find out how well his company is doing in comparison to others. He has one inspector for every 20 drivers, constantly checking on how things are going.

In short, his idea of a good manager is one who sets up a system, directs the work through subordinates and by making crisp and unambiguous assignments, develops a basis to set standards of performance for his employees. He sets goals and production targets. He rates employee performance objectively against these targets.[9]

Sounds like a well-run company, doesn't it? If you answered yes, you must read the rest of Dr. Tribus' article. Additionally, you must read every page of this book, Dr. Deming's book, and attend his four-day seminar. If you answered yes, your reasons may be very understandable. From the period just following World War II until recently, United States business has enjoyed a veritable monopoly when it came to large-scale manufacturing. As William Ouchi points out in his new book *The M-Form Society:*

We enjoyed forty years of an unprecedented industrial monopoly during which our companies earned monopoly profits, labor took home monopoly wages, and government extracted monopoly taxes...When there is such a monopoly, the stage is set for superstitious learning. Under monopoly, the management can be remiss and the workers can be inefficient, yet the company will have greater sales and earnings each year. Everyone concerned will "learn" that they know how to run the business and make money. That learning, however, is entirely superstitious and bears no relation to reality.[10]

Galileo, when he wanted to show his new invention, the telescope, to the astronomers of his day, was confronted with superstitious learning. They declined to see all of the new stars in the heavens because Aristotle had already told them how many there were.

It takes a big jolt for people to understand that the old philosophy will not be adequate in this new economic age, and still a bigger jolt to persuade them to accept the new philosophy. People are the same the world over. It takes a calamity to get their attention. Dr. Samuel Johnson said that nothing heightens a man's senses as the prospect of being hanged in the morning. Japan lost a military war; its people's backs were against the wall; their only resources were people and willing management. The United States, in many industrial segments, is losing an economic war. In some segments, it has already lost it. One segment that is still waging the battle is the automobile industry. Their management was not unlike other management: it took a calamity to get its attention. There is nothing like losing billions of dollars over a few short years to heighten a man's senses. Even so, the superstitious learning takes a long time to undo and then replace with the new philosophy. One element of the old way was the industry's preoccupation with watching each other. As long as they were all in the same ballpark playing the same game, all was well. In one particular parameter, "things gone wrong" from the customer's viewpoint, the industry was satisfied that they were all about equal when it came to complaints of customers. General Motors, Ford, and Chrysler would trade places year after year.

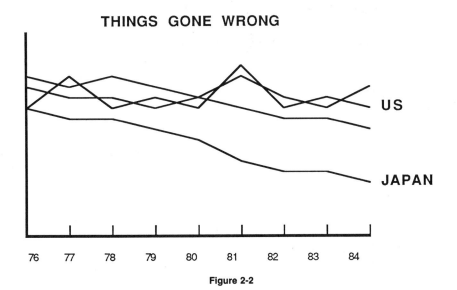

THINGS GONE WRONG

US

JAPAN

76 77 78 79 80 81 82 83 84

Figure 2-2

While the U.S. auto companies were preoccupied with looking at each other, the Japanese auto companies were busy looking after the needs of their customers. Year by year, the Japanese auto makers steadily improved. No real dramatic improvement, but clearly a pattern of continuing improvement. Clearly, the signal of a new economic age.

What is this new economic age? It centers around the statement: Higher quality costs less, not more.

Folklore has it in America that quality and production are incompatible: that you cannot have both. A plant manager will usually tell you that it is either or. In his experience, if he pushes quality, he falls behind in production. If he pushes production,

OUTMODED RELATIONSHIP

Figure 2-3

his quality suffers. This will be his experience when he knows not what quality is nor how to achieve it. A clear, concise answer came forth in a meeting with twenty-two production workers and union representatives, in response to the question: why is it that productivity increases as quality improves? The answer was a unanimous "less rework".

OUTMODED RELATIONSHIP

Figure 2-4

Emphasis on improvement of the process however increases uniformity of output of product, reduces rework and mistakes, reduces waste of manpower, machine-time, and materials and thus increases output with less effort and less cost. Other benefits of improved quality are lower costs, better competitive position, and happier people on the job, and more jobs, through better competitive position of the company.

Reduction of waste transfers man hours and machine hours from the manufacture of defectives into the manufacture of additional good product. In effect, the capacity of a production line is increased. The benefits of better quality through improve-

Tightening specifications results in more rework and more scrap

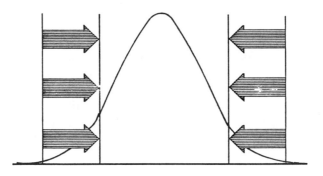

Figure 2-5

ment of the process are thus not just better quality, and the long-range improvement of market position that goes along with it, but greater productivity and much better profit as well. Improved morale of the work force is another gain: they now see that the management is making some effort themselves, and not blaming all faults on the production workers.

Some figures taken from experience will illustrate what happens. A schoolboy can understand them, but somehow management has not learned. The superintendent in a plant knew that there were problems with a certain production line. His only explanation was that the work force made a lot of mistakes. The first step was to get data from inspection and plot the fraction defective day by day over the past six weeks.

This plot, which is a run chart, showed stable random variation above and below the average (in other words, pretty good

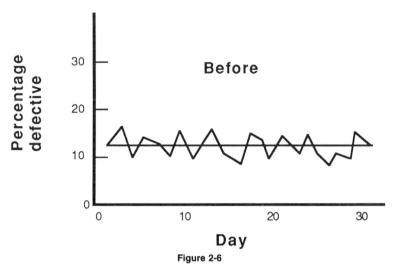

Day

Figure 2-6

statistical control). A stable system for production of defective items existed. What does this mean? It means that any substantial improvement must come from the system, the responsibility of management. This management had never used the figures from inspection. Hence the superintendent was totally unaware that the proportion defective here had been running along at eleven percent.

Should the superintendent have known that the proportion defective had been eleven percent? The answer to this question is always, no hesitation, a thunderous yes. Which is absolutely wrong! What could he have done with the figure had he known it? Probably tell his work force that eleven percent was unacceptable and that they had better do something to eliminate the mistakes or they would pay the consequences. The action that he would have taken would have been the same whether the proportion defective had been two percent, eleven percent, or seventeen percent. What is key here is the observation of statistical control, and that any substantial improvement must come from the system, which is management's responsibility. The fact that the level of defectives was eleven percent is incidental. The management had heretofore been unaware of any responsibility for quality. No one had ever used the figures from inspection. Actually, it was probably better for the company that management did not use the inspection figures because both quality and productivity would have suffered with the workers scurrying about trying to change things in response to management's exhortations when it was the system itself that needed change and could only be changed by management.

What could the management do? Dr. Deming made the suggestion, based on experience, that possibly the people on the job, and the inspector also, did not understand well enough what kind of work is acceptable and what is not. The manager and two supervisors eventually accepted this possibility and went to work on the matter. With trial and error they came up in seven weeks with operational definitions, with examples posted for everyone to see. A new set of data showed the proportion defective to be five percent.

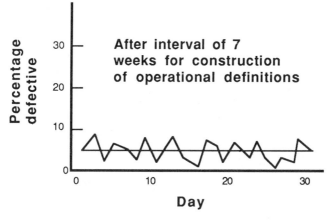

Figure 2-7

Before action was taken to improve the system, eleven dollars out of every one hundred were spent making defective units, while eighty-nine dollars were spent making good units. After improvement of the system, the average proportion defective had stablized at 5 percent. Ninety-five dollars were spent making good product and only five dollars were spent making defectives. The results are obvious:

- Quality is up
- Production of good product is up 6 percent
- Capacity is up 6 percent
- Cost per unit of good product is lower
- Profits are up
- The customer is happier
- Everybody is happier

The gains were immediate (7 weeks); the cost next to nothing:

same work force, same burden, no investment in new machinery. There still is a lot more improvement possible, however. That five percent must be reduced in order to successfully compete in this new economic age. What management now knows is that because the system is in statistical control, it is their responsibility, not their workers', to change the system. Because of it, people are working smarter, not harder.[2]

The adoption of anything new is difficult. Anything that calls for you to give up some of the precepts that you held as dogma is extremely difficult. One of the reasons that Dr. Deming's philosophy has not been widely adopted in America is that it calls for major change—revolution, if you will. Other prominent quality experts call for evolution, and have implied that management would not have to change too dramatically. It is a pity that people usually take the path of least resistance. Don Petersen, chairman of Ford Motor Company, is one executive who has recognized the need for change and has been outspoken in his continuing drive for quality. He opened a Deming Seminar in February 1982 with these words to some of Ford's most senior executives:

...As I was thinking about this meeting, it struck me strongly that you are the ones who are going to decide whether we are really successful in making a dramatic change in how we do business. You are the ones...It can be very difficult to make significant changes, especially when you have been in the habit of doing things differently for decades, and especially when the very success that brought you to the positions you now hold was rooted in doing some things, frankly, the wrong way. It is going to be hard for you to accept that—that you were promoted for the wrong reasons a time or two.

I seriously suggest that you give that some heartfelt thought as to whether you really understand what we are talking about. I had the experience in January at our Management Review, that most people in the room thought I was talking about something so elementary that we, of course, already do it in the Ford Motor Company. They could not understand why I was talking about it. It left me with the sense that many of us still do not understand what we are really trying to change. So I urge you to ask yourselves, do you really understand what it is we are trying to change...[11]

Mr. Petersen has realized that meaningful change can only take place from within. The problem is not with the competition. Although, as I stated earlier, the industry had become very accustomed to running their businesses by watching each other. In fact, many of them are still focusing on the competition, only this time it is Japan. In a few years it will be Korea, then China, then some other country. If you just try to meet the competition, you will not survive in this new economic age. You must try to meet the customer, not just the competition. And it is you who must change, not the competition.

Chapter 3

Cease dependence on inspection to achieve quality. Eliminate the need for inspection on a mass basis by building quality into the product in the first place. (Point 3)

Every one of us in business manages processes. Every one of us has customers and suppliers, and every one of us is a customer and a supplier. We all affect the quality of what the ultimate customer purchases. In its simplest form, a process is a blending or a transformation of inputs such as people, materials, equipment, methods, and environment into outcomes. Some of these inputs do the transforming and some of them are transformed. (I am very grateful to Dr. Edward Baker for the refinements in the process model.$_{12}$)

PROCESS DEFINITION

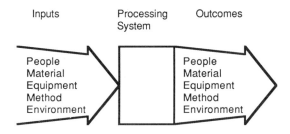

Figure 3-1

In a business organization, many processes are interrelated and one process' product or service is another's input. One processing system's inputs might come from one or several processing systems' outcomes. These outcomes might be invoices, waiting time for service, a camshaft, engineering design changes, a trained employee, or a myriad of other possibilities.

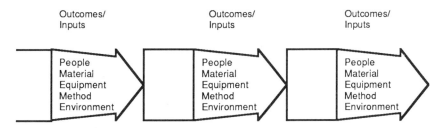

Figure 3-2

The customer does not have to be a person, either. It could be the next machine receiving the output material. It could be the institution receiving a report or procedure. It might be the environment receiving effluents. It could take the form of any of the other resources: material, method, equipment, or environment.

Some processes are people-dominant. That is, the people contribute the most to the variability of the outcomes. Other processes might be material or method or equipment or environment-dominant. In still others, no one input will obviously dominate.

The old, expensive way of doing business is to try to manage the outcomes by detecting defects. In this system, detection of defects is accomplished by the method of mass inspection, sending the supposedly good product on to the customer, while either scrapping or reworking the supposedly bad product. The flow of resources is one way, from producer to consumer. It is the old way of doing business (design it, make it, sell it) as Dr. Deming described it in Chapter 1. You might be able to give the customer good quality, but it will be at a relatively high cost. There is the added cost of the mass inspection, which can be considerable. In addition, there is the cost of dissatisfied customers because mass inspection, as usually carried out, ships some bad items and sends for rework or scrap some of the good ones.

THE PROCESS USED FOR THE DETECTION OF DEFECTS

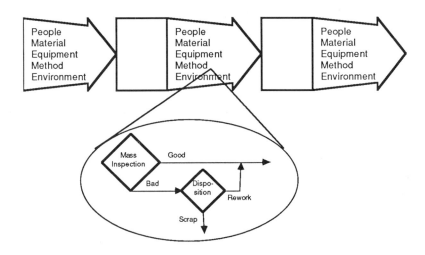

Figure 3-3

In order to make this point, I want you to participate in a process which thousands of people have done before you. It is the process of proofreading. You are the people. Use whatever method you choose. Your material is the highlighted sentence. The characteristic which is critical to the customer is the number of f's in the sentence. Read the sentence and note exactly how many occurrences of the letter "f" you see.

FINISHED FILES ARE THE RESULT
OF YEARS OF SCIENTIFIC STUDY
COMBINED WITH THE
EXPERIENCE
OF MANY YEARS

Figure 3-4

Many people see exactly three f's. Many people see exactly six f's. A few people see two, four, five, seven, and even zero f's. (Actually the only people who saw zero f's were those who were given a blank sheet of paper because of a copy machine malfunction. I don't hand out this test on paper any more!) There are two lessons to be learned here. The first one is that teaching adults is a lot more difficult in many ways than teaching children. Each of you brings with you the length and breadth of your experience and knowledge. You were carefully taught many things. You were carefully taught how to read English. Most of us learned to read the language phonetically. This seems to be true whether you learned English as a first, second, or third language. This could explain the results of those who saw exactly three f's (approximately 40 percent). The f in the word "of" sounds like a v and people typically skip over it. Those who saw exactly six f's (approximately 50 percent) were probably using a different method. Some read backwards or force themselves to scan each letter and not read the words. The reasons for those who saw other than six or three (approximately 10 percent) have not been scientifically explained. In any event, only about half the people were able to meet the customers' needs. As you read this book or Dr. Deming's book, you need to realize that some of what you learned about how to manage might be, as Professor Ouchi says, "superstitious" learning. Dr. Deming's philosophy will cause you to question your learning. Approach it with an open mind. The methods you should be using to manage might not be what you now think they are.

Which brings me to the important second point: in spite of what you have learned, attempting to detect defects through mass inspection is not good enough. This was a very simple process where the kind of defect (the letter f) was probably understood uniformly by all. Think how much more variability there will be in processes in which the needs of the customer are not as simple. Detection of defects, even with the use of sophisticated technology, is not a viable competitive strategy in this new economic age. If you have been on the shop or factory floor you know this. Take some parts that have just been passed by an automatic inspection machine. Throw them in the hopper; some of them now will fail the test. By the same token, take some parts that have just failed an automatic inspection. Throw them in the hopper, and some of them now pass the test.[13]

Some companies have found a way to take advantage of the uncertainties of mass inspection and greatly reduce their administrative costs as well. The customer buys a rubber stamp which reads:

Figure 3-5

while the supplier has one which reads:

We have
reinstructed
the operator and it
won't happen again

Figure 3-6

It is a version of administrative ping-pong. If you are to play a game, it should not cost an arm and a leg. The game that they are really playing is Russian Roulette with the ultimate customer. The stakes are a lot more than an arm and a leg.

As you have seen, detection of defects is not a viable competitive strategy in this new economic age. There is a better way. Improve the process to prevent the occurrence of defects.

In a process used for prevention, the same five types of inputs are transformed into outcomes. But instead of dependence on mass inspection of those outcomes after they were made, the prevention use of the process incorporates feedback from the process itself and from the customer to change the process inputs before the outcomes are produced. Statistical methods can play an important part in a process used for prevention of defects. But many times they are misused (more on that in Chapter 11). In reality, we don't often see use of a process for only the purposes of detection or only the purposes of prevention (Pete Jessup pointed this out to me). It is usually a mixture of feed-forward detection and feedback prevention. Well-meaning companies (and especially companies trying to do business

THE PROCESS USED FOR THE PREVENTION OF
DEFECTS

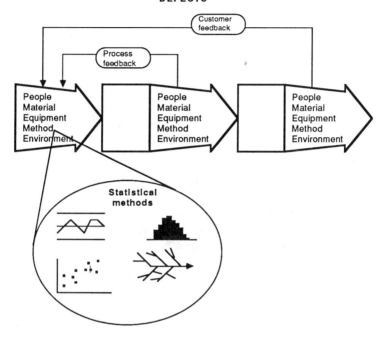

Figure 3-7

with the government) often bear the costs of both. One costly misuse that I
often see arises from confusion between data from the customer feedback
loop and the process feedback loop. Most people recognize the need to reduce
the feedback-to-action time frame wherever possible. They see that warranty
data are often too late to take immediate action and thus establish inspection
and feedback not only to reduce warranty, but also to anticipate it. In their
zeal to nip defects in the bud, management has more and more turned
solely to technology as the answer.

Automatic compensating machinery has extremely fast feedback but is the
epitome of the misuse of a detection/prevention process because it typically
reacts to individual readings. Because it reacts to individual readings, and
not to statistical signal, the process variance can be twice as much with this
kind of feedback as without it. Attendees of Dr. Deming's seminar will
recognize the doubling of variance in this automatic compensation example
as Rule Two in the Nelson Funnel Experiment. An actual example follows.

An input shaft in a transmission was turned in a machine equipped with an
automatic compensation device. The manufacturer had programmed the
device to check a particular diameter on every piece. The program compen-
sated the tool after each measurement in an amount equal to the deviation

from the specification midpoint. If we look at a consecutive 50-piece run with the compensating device activated, we see that the output stayed uniformly spread within the specifications.

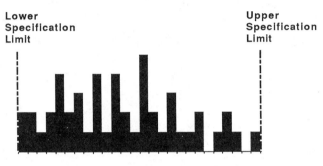

Figure 3-8

If we next look at a consecutive 50-piece run with the compensating device turned off, we see that the output spread is greatly reduced.

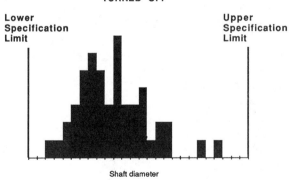

Figure 3-9

The point here is that new, expensive technology is not in itself the answer to quality and productivity deficiences. As most factories modernize in the 80's and 90's, manufacturers have an opportunity to differentiate the way they produce their goods, even though they all will be using the same types of microprocessor base equipment. The way to differentiate production is through intelligent programming.[14]

The waste of overcontrol occurs because management does not understand that the world is variable. The manager that Dr. Deming wrote about in the previous chapter thought that if everyone did as he were told, everything would be right.

Even if the people, equipment, materials, methods, and environment all stay the same within limits as narrow as anyone could specify, will the outcomes be the same?

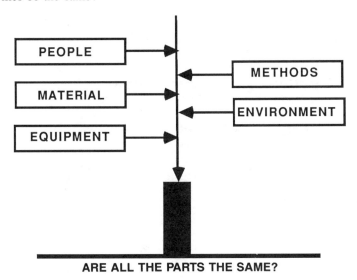

ARE ALL THE PARTS THE SAME?

Figure 3-10

We, in fact, know that the outcomes will not be the same: they will vary.
Any process contains many sources of variability. There is no such thing as strict constancy. Differences between products may be large, or they may be almost unmeasurably small, but they are always present...Some sources of variation in the process cause very short-run piece-to-piece differences—e.g., backlash and clearances within a machine and its fixturing, or the accuracy of a bookkeeper's work. Other sources of variation cause changes in the output only over a longer period of time, either gradually as with tool or machine wear, step-wise as with procedural changes, or irregularly, as with environmental changes such as power surges or illness.[15]

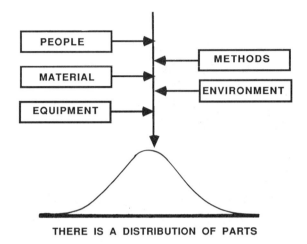

THERE IS A DISTRIBUTION OF PARTS

Figure 3-11

As these outcomes accumulate, they may be described by their location, spread, and shape.

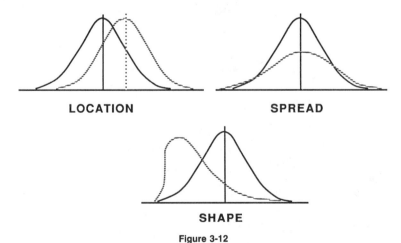

LOCATION   **SPREAD**

SHAPE

Figure 3-12

So without changing anything or adjusting anything in the process, there will be variability in the outcomes. Because of variability, there is a chance that an outcome could occur at location 2 in the right-hand tail of the distribution, as in Figure 3-13.

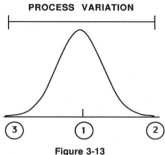

Figure 3-13

The automatic compensating equipment, or, for that matter, a very conscientious worker, is really assuming that the process has changed and adjusts the location of the process an equivalent distance to the left, in this case from location 1 to location 3 (as in Figure 3-14). Because of this adjustment, outcomes even further to the left are now possible, whereas they were not if the process had just been left alone. The next reading could have been anywhere inside the original distribution.

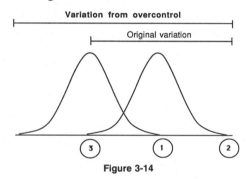

Figure 3-14

By extension, we see that the variance of the outcomes can be doubled by a policy of adjusting to every reading.

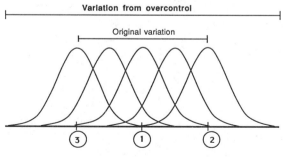

Figure 3-15

We need to understand, in the broad business context, how overcontrol can be so costly. First of all, as much as management says that they understand how reacting to every reading on the shop floor can double the variance, they have a tougher time understanding that they, too, manage processes, and if they demand to know why costs went up a tenth of a point over last period or why sales went down or why first-run capability went down or why warranty claims went up, and they expect action on these variations, then they are guilty of overcontrol and the associated high costs of doing business that way. Your people will have answers to explain the change because they like to stay employed. But the answers will have about as much relevance as the explanations we get each day on why the stock market went up or down.

I have seen solutions to overcontrol. The spouse of a friend of mine was always adjusting the house thermostat. It was either too hot or too cold. The resultant variability of the inside temperature drove him to surreptitiously disconnect the existing thermostat (he rewired and hid the new one) so that his wife might adjust it to her heart's content.

Reaction to individual reading increases variability of the outcomes. Management might say that they can live with variability as long as the outcomes meet specifications or satisfy procedures. Just to meet the specifications is a high-cost way of doing business, as I shall show in the next chapter.

As much as prevention of defects is an improvement over the detection of defects, it is still an attributes-type system. That is, you either have a defect or you do not have a defect. The emphasis is on managing the outcomes and not necessarily the process. With both of these approaches you may be able to "do it right the first time" or get zero defects or meet specifications or get no warranty claims or get zero complaint letters from the customer. But there is a big difference between getting no complaints and having people brag about using your products and services. A very big difference. The lack of a negative does not mean that there is a strong positive.

It pays to keep the customers satisfied: If a car owner likes his car, he's apt to buy four more cars of the same make over the following twelve years, says Technical Assistance Research Program, a Washington consulting firm that specializes in consumer behavior. The customer is also likely to spread the good news to eight other people. But woe to the car company that delivers a shoddy product. An angry car buyer will tell his troubles to an average of sixteen people.[16]

What leads or persuades people to brag about using your products and services? Identifying their needs and expectations and then consistently meeting them. How do you do that? Through looking ahead, to outguess the customer; to provide years from now what will appeal to the customer. Through the process of continuous improvement.

Chapter 4

Improve constantly and forever the system of production and service, to improve quality and productivity, and thus constantly decrease costs. (Point 5)

The Process of Continuous Improvement spirals toward a customer target. Improvement is possible because integral to the process is the Deming Cycle. (He calls it the Shewhart Cycle, some know it as the Plan, Do, Check, Act or PDCA Cycle. You saw the first iteration of it in Chapter 1 which was excerpted from a transcript of Dr. Deming's lectures to the Japanese in 1950.) It is in this process of Continuous Improvement that several important precepts of the Deming philosophy are manifested. I will highlight them as I explain the process.

The Deming cycle is a procedure for the improvement of analytical (see Chapter 11) problems or opportunities. There are four steps in the procedure that occur over time.

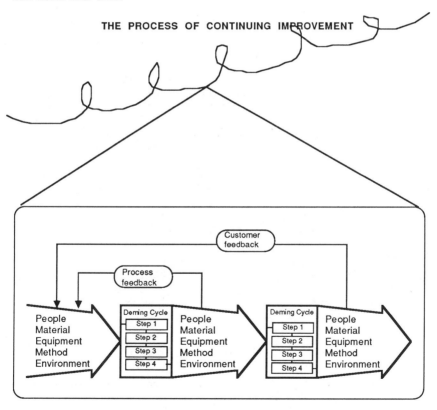

THE PROCESS OF CONTINUING IMPROVEMENT

DEMING CYCLE

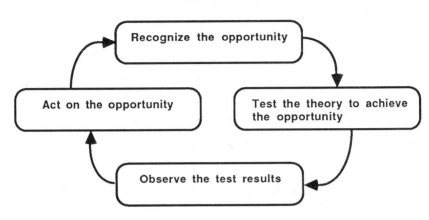

Figure 4-2

Step. 1. Recognize the Opportunity.
   Step 1a. Operationally Define the Opportunity.

Step 1a. Operationally define the opportunity

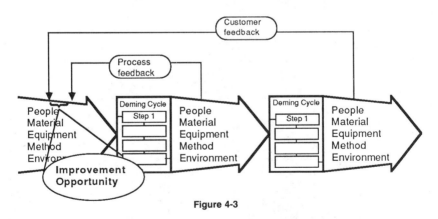

Figure 4-3

The opportunity for improvement in this customer-driven process can be thought of as the gap between the customer's needs expressed through the Customer Feedback loop and the process performance expressed through the Process Feedback loop. (This is another way of looking at or describing the capability of a process.) The opportunity to improve diminishes (or the capability of the process increases) as the two get closer and closer together and the process variability gets smaller and smaller. Later in this chapter I will more fully explain this vital aspect of the process of Continuous Improvement. It makes it possible to have higher quality at lower cost.

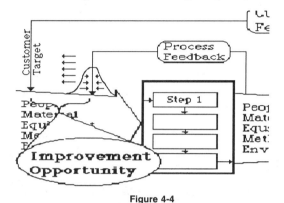

Figure 4-4

Now in order to meet the customer's needs, we must first know them and operationally define them as described in Chapter 1. This means that we must get the customer and the supplier involved in understanding what the customer wants. This step could start with only the perception of an opportunity, but must be followed by an operational definition. When this is done, we can proceed to operationally define the theory on how to realize the opportunity.

Step 1b. Operationally Define the Theory.

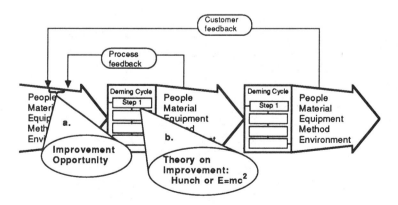

Figure 4-5

The theory could start with a hunch or it could be as certain as a law of nature or physics. The result should not only be the statement of the theory but also the plan by which the theory is tested. The only purpose of collecting data or conducting an experiment or test is to form the basis of a rational prediction. Dr. Deming has said that anyone may predict anything that he wishes. But he is only interested in rational predictions. That is to say, those predictions that have roots based in theory. It is important to make your predictions before the experiment is conducted because too many people can "prove" anything afterward. Dr. Deming tosses a coin in the air, lets it land, looks at it and calls "heads." He says that he cannot get people to play with him because he makes his predictions afterwards.

Step 2. Test the Theory.

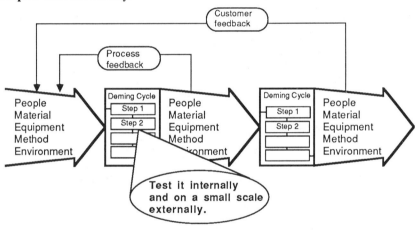

Figure 4-6

You should carry out the test in the laboratory or production setting (office or factory) and on a small scale with your customers. You should test it on your customers for two reasons. One, their satisfaction might be increased by your educating them. And two, you can always improve your understanding of what you think they want.

Step 3. Observe the Results.

Statistical Methods can obviously be of help here as you analyze the results. But you must be observant of anything, quantitative or qualitative, which could affect your ability to predict tomorrow's results.

Step 3. Observe the results

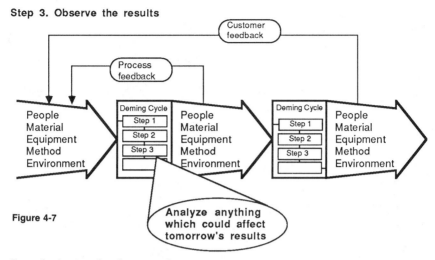

Figure 4-7

Step 4. Act on the Opportunity.

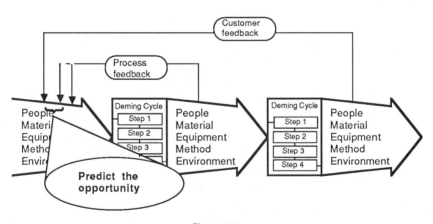

Figure 4-8

The prediction that you made in Step 1 can be modified as a result of what you have learned from the test you conducted to verify your theory. You cannot put any probability on what you learned, but you can build up a reasonable degree of belief in your prediction. (See Chapter 11 for further details.) You should then act on what you learned in the experiment. In this step, and in fact in any of the steps, you might want to cycle through the process so that the outcome is the implemented result of the experiment. In other words, you will find yourself nesting the various steps of the Process of Continuous Improvement.

The next step is a repeat of Step 1 in which you test what you implemented with your previous operational definition of the opportunity. The other steps are then followed until the team feels that they should go on to some other opportunity that has meanwhile become more important. What you should remember is to continually cycle through each of the steps. Sometimes, if nothing has changed, you won't dwell too long on Step 1. Nevertheless, you must think through this step because the planning that results from it is usually short-circuited in favor of doing something and then having to do it over. It seems that people, many times, opt for spending $10 four times instead of $25 once.

Some theories on improvement.

There is potential for improvement in each step that we take to create products and services. This is a strict departure from traditional learning that some level of control or performance is good enough. An excellent example of this difference in the manufacturing aspect of our business is our historical acceptance of the fact that meeting engineering specifications was the best one could do in providing a quality product.

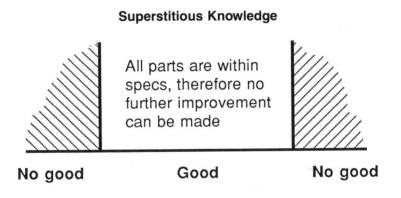

Superstitious Knowledge

All parts are within specs, therefore no further improvement can be made

No good   Good   No good

Figure 4-9

This superstitious learning is not good enough anymore, especially in international markets, if we are to consistently meet our customers' needs, and if we are to get them to brag about owning our products. Instead, we must continually reduce the variability of our products and services thus obtaining the highest quality at the lowest cost.

CONTINUALLY REDUCE THE VARIABILITY

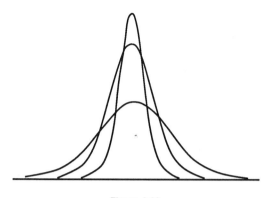

Figure 4-10

An excellent example of the benefits of continuous improvement was shown in the manufacturing of an automatic transmission for front-wheel-drive automobiles. The transmissions were produced from the same blueprints by two different sources: a plant in the United States and a plant in Japan. Some similarities and some differences were observed:

● While both plants met the engineering specifications, the Japanese transmissions used less than 30% of the tolerance and the American ones used about 70% of the tolerance.

● This piece-to-piece consistency resulted in warranty costs that were one third lower for the parts from Japan. This was on top of a unit manufacturing cost which was significantly less.

The message was clear: higher quality costs less, not more. The U.S. plant manager then proceeded to apply this knowledge to his processes. One such process involved the manufacture of an idler gear. The quality of the transmission (as perceived by the customer due to transmission noise) is affected by this particular gear. One important characteristic of this part is the squareness of the gear. That is, the relationship between the outer and inner diameters to the gear face. An out-of-square condition could cause gear noise that might be objectionable to vehicle occupants. In order to minimize this possibility, the input, output, and idler gear were processed to be matched and assembled as a set. The plant launched an effort to produce gears better than the engineering specifications and see if this increased consistency would result in decreased total cost.

The result was a substantial improvement in a relatively short period of time. Since the goal was not to simply meet specifications, once capability to consistently produce parts within specifications was achieved, further reduction in the variation of output became the focus. The results were extremely convincing:

● First, incidence of gear noise complaints received from customers has been reduced from its already low level to virtually none.

● Second, as the variation of squareness of the input gear was now stabilized at a very low level, the need for gear matching was eliminated. The gear matching operation has been dropped, thus lowering the cost of manufacturing.

● Third, the scheduled periodic chuck maintenance was dropped and now maintenance is only performed when the control charts indicate that it is necessary.

● Fourth, scrap was reduced substantially to virtually nothing.

● Fifth, the need for 100% final inspection of the input gear squareness has been eliminated. The output is now predictably stable and the inspection step has been dropped.[17]

Notice that because quality has improved, so has productivity. Customers are happier with the products, and the cost of doing business is less, not more. What is important to realize here is that truly competitive improvement can be made only if management has the flexibility to increase costs in some areas. The customer cares about total cost. So should the manager. If you have a system which expects uniform savings out of each department or organization, you might be suboptimizing yourself out of business. By spending a little more money in one area, you might be able to greatly reduce your total cost. This reduction of total cost is the primary reason why continuous improvement is an essential business strategy.

Continuous improvement will cost less if it is done right. Dr. Deming planted the seeds for continuous improvement in Japan in 1950. These ideas were codified by Genichi Taguchi in 1960. The description presented here follows the excellent clarifying work done by Peter T. Jessup in 1983.[18] Again, we have to challenge some superstitious learning. That learning said that we pay no economic loss if the parts are inside the engineering tolerances, but we pay all of the economic cost if the parts are outside.

**STEPFUNCTION INTERPRETATION
OF LOSS**

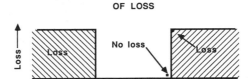

Figure 4-11

In reality, what is the difference between a part just inside the engineering tolerances and one just outside? None, because our management systems are very accommodating. In the short term, if the foreman needs it for his quota, the part gets shipped. If there is more time, he can get an engineering deviation and the parts get shipped. In this new economic age, however, you can nickel and dime yourself into extinction. Dr. Deming states that in business, you can get beaten up a lot or a little, depending on your actions. But as I mentioned in previous chapters, history is replete with examples of society accepting the accumulation of small losses and rallying to avoid one large loss which, in reality, might be smaller than the total of the smaller losses. The point is that the underlying model of engineering tolerances does not support real-world experiences. I once heard George Box say, "All models are wrong. Some models are useful." The step-function model has been faithfully used for years, but in this new economic age, there is a more useful model. And that model takes the form of a parabola, not a step-function. Now, the issue is not whether the loss is exactly quadratic, the issue is that the quadratic model is a lot closer to the real world than the step function. You might, when you are fine tuning your process after a few iterations of the Process of Continuous Improvement, spend time to determine more closely the loss function of your specific customers. But for the most part, I would just proceed with the quadratic approximation.

We need to change our learning to recognize that there is an economic loss for any deviation from a target value, a value that will lead the customer to praise the product. That loss may be small for slight deviations from the target, but it gets larger the further away from the target the outcome is. This model more closely agrees with the real world in that there really is not much difference between a point just inside the engineering tolerances and one just outside. These losses are downstream losses because of future problems, such as parts not assembled smoothly, lost opportunities because of delays, lack of consistency because of no operational definitions, warranty or customer complaint costs, and even loss because customers are not praising the product. Some of these losses are visible, as Dr. Deming says, and some are invisible.

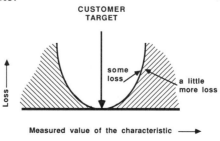

Figure 4-12

If you are going to run a competitive business today, you must balance the visible and the invisible figures. If you manage solely on gut feelings or your experience, you won't be competitive. If you manage solely on visible figures you won't be competitive. Dr. Deming has said many times, "He who runs his company on visible figures alone will soon have neither company nor visible figures to work with." People have a tendency to look at a visible figure and to run with it without really understanding its limitations. Realizing this, I am going to use some visible figures. But, I am also going to fulfill my responsibility of letting you know their limitations. First of all, every process has its own set of downstream losses due to variability. And second, while I am going to use a visible figure, there are other invisible figures affecting the downstream losses of the process. So, for explanatory purposes, the loss at the specification limits is one dollar.

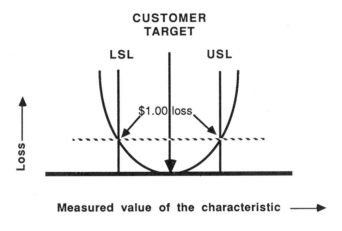

CUSTOMER TARGET

Figure 4-13

That is one dollar for each unit produced. The loss does not have to be symmetrical. It could be one dollar at the upper spec and a dollar and fifty cents at the lower spec. In this example, however, the loss is the same at both specification limits. I define specification limits as the point of economic indifference between the loss incurred downstream and the cost to replace or repair the unit.

We are now ready to look at what this means in this world. We will first look at a process that is capable. By this I mean that after stability (statistical control) is established, nearly all the distribution of individual parts falls inside the engineering tolerances. (I am also making an assumption that is never fully realized in the real world; the assumption being that individual parts are normally distributed.)

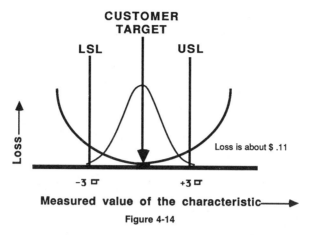

Figure 4-14

We see that if the emphasis is on the engineering tolerances, essentially we will not make any defective products; we are doing it right the first time. There is no economic loss because we are meeting the engineering tolerances. But if we look at it from the perspective that we are paying an economic penalty for every deviation from a target value, we see that there is a hidden opportunity in this example of about eleven cents (in other words, 11% because we normalized the unit cost and loss at the specification limits to $1.00) which can be spent on the process to reduce its variabililty so that more people are praising our product or service. In Figure 4-14, the area is representative of the actual loss, which really is the integration of the loss function and the distribution of individual outcomes ($\int L(x) f(x)dx$). At this point we need to be reminded of Dr. Deming's view on quality that recognizes value to the customer, not quality at any cost. In the above situation, it would be bad management to spend 20% to fix an 11% loss. (I purposely did not say 12% because that would imply a precision that does not exist in the real world.)

Let us say that you were able to improve the process (by spending up to about 11%) so that it is now plus or minus ten standard deviations of the distribution of individual outcomes. This would be, by any standard, a very capable process.

In this case, the loss, if centered on this target, would be about one percent. What do we typically see when a process is this capable? Well, one of the things we see is a tendency not to try to correct special cases. After all, we are so far from the engineering tolerances and we are not going to make any bad pieces. You will, however, pay for that decision in the marketplace. Another thing that we see is the manufacturing practice of

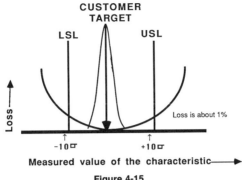

Figure 4-15

letting the process drift between the engineering tolerances. We have tool wear problems and constant pressure to keep the machines running, and if the rule is to just stay within the engineering tolerances, this practice would make sense. We are really not making any bad parts; why should we do better? Again, we will pay for that decision in the marketplace. Management is paid to manage total costs. The customer doesn't care if our tool costs are low. He cares about the total value that he gets out of his product or service. So by trying to save on tool costs, look at what the real cost to the customer is due to the increased variation.

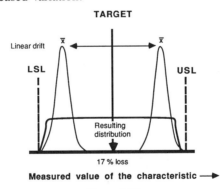

Figure 4-16

Instead of losing one percent, we now lose 17%. That is worse than the just capable normal process which only lost 11%. Overcontrol can get you the same uniform spread within the specifications, not making any defective products, but costing a lot of money in the marketplace. You want people praising to others about owning your product or service, not just not complaining.

If the process of continuous improvement will get people to praise your product or service, what is preventing you from doing it? Roadblocks abound on the path of Continuous Improvement.

Chapter 5

Remove barriers that rob the hourly worker of his right to pride of workmanship. The responsibility of supervisors must be changed from stressing sheer numbers to quality. Remove barriers that rob people in management and engineering of their right to pride of workmanship. This means, inter alia, abolishment of the annual merit rating and of management by objective. (Point 12)

If management really wants to meet customers' needs and expectations, if they really want to have their customers bragging, they must first take the lead in examining every management system and operating procedure to determine if it supports or inhibits continuing improvement. Some of the systems are obvious. Dr. Deming specifically mentions work standards (Point 11), training (Points 6 and 13), and purchasing (Point 4). But there are a host of other inhibiting systems which are not so obvious. They are not obvious because management does not understand statistical thinking; they do not understand the reality of variation. And this is especially critical because only top management can change these inhibiting systems. So as soon as top management asks:

"What do you want me to do?"

You tell them to first learn about variability, and then to begin to change company systems. They won't be expecting that answer. I have found that they are more than willing (well, some more than others) to spend money on training their people, or to commission the development of a case study, or to buy some new technology. But it is always for someone else. Even though it is for their organization, it is not personally for them. But if management really expects to meet their customers' needs at a price that the customers are willing to pay, they must change company systems. They need to personally understand that this is for them. As part of this change, they must recognize that there are some things that their people do today that they shouldn't be doing tommorrow. Management has a history of adding on programs to an already full plate. They must decide what has to go in order to make room for the new systems.

In this chapter, I will cover three of the systems that I consider to be major inhibitors. They are the following:

● Performance Appraisal System
● Daily Production Reports
● Financial Management System

1. Performance Appraisal System.

This system is the biggest inhibitor to continuing improvement in any organization. Wherever it is used, there are at least five major reasons why the traditional performance appraisal system is an inhibitor to continuing improvement. It

- destroys teamwork
- fosters mediocrity
- increases variability
- confounds the people with the other input resources, and
- focuses on the short term.

The performance appraisal system destroys teamwork. American businesses are functionally oriented. They have purchasing, engineering, manufacturing, finance, marketing, and other functional departments. Each discipline is evaluated on objectives which are again functionally oriented. For instance, high on purchasing's list of good things to do is to lower negotiated cost. High on manufacturing's list is to reduce warranty. High on engineering's list is to reduce weight (at least in the automotive industry). As the system works, these are mutually exclusive goals. A manufacturing manager might want to use a different kind of bearing because he is being charged with high warranty costs on the current bearing. If the manager gets the new bearing he needs to meet his objective, a buyer might not meet his objective of negotiating lower costs because the new bearing costs two dollars more than the current one. Additionally, nothing is in it for engineering because they have already met their weight objective. Obviously, any of the positions in this scenario can change and the resultant built-in conflict still exists. Now there is some cooperation, but it is in spite of the system, not because of it. The buyer might cooperate with the plant manager because they are friends. But if it means not meeting his objective, the cooperation predictably ends. His bonus, his raise, his blemish-free career, his family's security all depend on him meeting his objectives, not others meeting theirs or the plant manager meeting his. This is a rational reaction to the system. It is not because people are inherently bad. In fact, I am starting with the premise that people are inherently good, that they want to take pride in their work.

Dr. Deming tells of two scientists who coauthored a research paper. They closely cooperated with each other to produce a paper that was much better than if each had done separate papers. When it was written, their management said that only one could go to the conference to present it, and the person to go would be the one with the higher performance rating. Can you think of a quicker way to dry up teamwork?

In another example, there had been some progress made in fostering interdivisional cooperation. These were internal customer/supplier relationships. Just as this cooperation was beginning to flourish, a "quality organization of the year" award was offered by a major university to the organization showing the most progress toward quality improvement. Almost immediately, the cooperation between divisions dried up. Each division wanted to win the award. Each division was afraid that their ideas would be stolen by the others. Each division proceeded alone to develop a case study to show their improvement. Each division lost the external competition. They lost it because of excessive internal competition.

An example I see all too often in American industry is the reality of the boss being the employee's most important customer. You look at the most publicized process flow diagram (Chapter 11) which is the organization chart, and you see that the main customer/supplier relationships are vertical.

- You must produce 5,000 widgets this week to meet your supervisor's quota, not a lesser but better amount to satisfy the assembly plant.
- Your boss gives you an "assignment" to explain the difference between this month's warranty figures and last month's. This means that you must put off meeting your other customer's need for more reliable parts.
- Your boss says that you have enough to do to meet this department's objectives and don't need to spend your time helping other departments. (Even though, by going upstream and helping other departments who supply you with needed inputs, you will be able to more efficiently meet the company's objectives.)

When the boss is the most important customer, other customers (those who use the employee's process outcomes) might be shortchanged and teamwork short circuited.

In each of these examples, there is a win-lose conflict built into the system. We need to develop a system where there is a win-win relationship between parties so that, as Ouchi states: There is "...a balance between individual entrepreneurship on the one hand and teamwork on the other."[19]

The performance appraisal system fosters mediocrity. Another way of saying this is that it reduces initiative or risk-taking. This is because it is an attributes-type system. That is, you either make your objective or you do not make your objective. The process typically begins when your boss proposes ambitious objectives and leaves you to make a proposal or statement on how difficult it will be to meet them. You do this because of fear of failure of meeting an objective. This fear is subtle, but very real. Industry has a history of replacing or reassigning employees who have not met their objectives. Mediocre objectives are the result of this negotiating process. You cannot compete in this new economic age if you foster this mediocrity. Some companies purposely set objectives that are easy to achieve because they want everybody to feel like a winner. If you work this way and that is all your people achieve, you might find it difficult to meet your customers' needs at a price they are willing to pay.

Another factor which contributes to lack of stretch is fear of the unknown.

You may know of ways to achieve an 8% savings right now. Your objective over the next two years is 10% (5% each year). What does your company see at the end of the first year? It sees 5%. Or maybe 5.1%, because then you will be able to claim that you exceeded your objective. You are effectively banking the additional 3% for next year so that the next objective can be met. It is what I call an Alexeyev mentality. You may recall that Vasili Alexeyev was a Russian superheavyweight weight lifter. He was given a reward for each world record that he broke. He knew exactly what to do— he broke a lot of world records. But he broke them a gram or two at a time! We need business systems which will foster continuing improvement, not stifle it. The problem is not the people, it is the system. People learn to survive in the system. And you cannot blame them for trying to do so.

I have observed engineers who have learned to play the system to meet yearly cost and weight objectives. It is a challenge to come up with a realistic but high figure for initial weight and cost characteristics so that there is enough fat to make yearly improvement objectives. Since engineers spend only around a third of their time on engineering tasks right now, we don't need systems that take up more of their time. Another highly visible objective for engineering is meeting the various project or program milestones. I have observed that the very visible milestones are met by delivery of blueprints or design specifications or bills of material, etc. The engineer gets credit for meeting another objective. But has he really met it? He delivered the drawings all right, but will he have to submit a change order at a later date because he didn't really deliver what his customer needed? The system gives him gold stars for meeting milestones. The other qualities of the deliverable are seldom mentioned except to say, "Of course I wanted good drawings."

Dr. Deming tells about the federal mediator who is evaluated on the number of meetings that he mediates as well as the number of settlements reached. He can get a higher rating if he takes more meetings to get a settlement. The waste is obvious, and also inexcusable.

Manufacturing representatives quickly learn that the way to get a good evaluation, as well as to keep their jobs, is not to let their customers buy too much from them. Sounds ridiculous, right? Well this mediocrity is nurtured by the fact that if a customer bought a large enough quantity of whatever the manufacturing rep was selling, then the customer might hire his own buyer, and the rep would lose an account.[20]

Purchasing organizations in the automotive industry waste untold man-hours worrying about dimensioning the labor cost difference between Japan and the United States. One of the prime motives for this frenetic activity is to document their cost reductions vis-a-vis the Japanese to get a better annual rating. The preoccupation of only looking at your competition dies hard in

Detroit.

It increases the variability of performance of people. This is because of the implied preciseness of the rating schemes. Traditional systems try to overly differentiate performance levels. As a result, we end up with categories such as outstanding high, outstanding, outstanding low, excellent high,

OUTSTANDING HIGH
OUTSTANDING
OUTSTANDING LOW
EXCELLENT HIGH
EXCELLENT
EXCELLENT LOW
SATISFACTORY HIGH
SATISFACTORY
SATISFACTORY LOW
UNSATISFACTORY

Figure 5-1

excellent, excellent low, satisfactory high, satisfactory, satisfactory low, unsatisfactory, and so on.

This implied preciseness or ranking, management feels, lets people know where they stand. The fact is, however, that you cannot define operationally the difference between any two adjacent categories. So, depending on perceived quotas or other pressures, the manager can always back into any rationalization to support the category he chose for you.

The military, and specifically the Navy, goes out of its way to let its officers know exactly where they stand vis-a-vis their peers in a Command. Each officer knows in which one of nine categories he is rated. He also

Mission Contribution	Not obs.	High			Mid		Low		Unsat
EVALUATION		X							
SUMMARY		2	3	1	0	0	0	0	0

Figure 5-2

knows in which categories his peers were placed.

The effect can be extremely devastating. Many times this pigeon-holing or binning makes it easier for management to determine rewards. The criteria for those prizes revolve around the assumption that we will reward those who are above average, or perhaps in the upper 1% or 5%, and in the most positive light encourage those in the lower half or bottom 90% to do better. The reason that management will reward those in these categories is that they feel that the differences in the categories are discernible. But did you know that in any group of ten people, one will be in the top 10% and one will be in the bottom 10%, and there is not a thing you can do about it. That will be the case before you ever begin. In all but the most extreme situations, about half will be above average and about half will be below average, and there is nothing you can do about it. Someone must be below average and someone must be above average. This reality, surprisingly, is not known by many in management. Consider the statement by the Nuclear Regulatory Commission that fifteen nuclear power plants were below average in overall performance and that they were going to make sure that their future inspections focused on the plants showing below average performance.[21] Consider learned historians making the following conclusions:

We've been remarkably lucky, considering the relatively haphazard way we select a president. Historians have determined that almost one out of every four has been great or near great, and over half are above average.[22]

Dr. Deming tells of a zone manager having three dealers; one of them is below average and is under extreme pressure to get to be above average. Some will be below and some will be above and there is NOTHING that anyone can do about it.

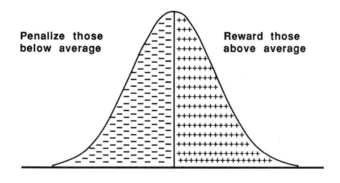

Figure 5-3

Many of the perceived differences in people really come from the other incoming resources of the process. The same process that puts a person above average one year might put him below average the next. Nobody really likes to be classified as below average. However, the way management has been avoiding its responsibilities to openly and honestly coach its people, below average now is "outstanding low!"

Performance appraisals are ineffective, inaccurate, unnecessary and often embarrassing, according to two surveys of more than 400 companies. Both surveys found that a major failure of performance reviews is an inability of managers to communicate with subordinates about their strengths and weaknesses.[23]

I have observed that the inability (or unwillingness) of managers to communicate with subordinates starts with the top management. The higher up you go in an organization, the more you are likely to fill out your own evaluation (actually everything except the summary category). Top management assumes that if you made it this far, you should know how you are doing, and they don't need to waste time filling out the paperwork. In fact, at the highest levels, the personnel department fills them in for you.

"Bracket creep" is one of the main reasons companies change their evaluation systems. When almost everyone ends up in the highest category, your career more heavily depends on the ability of your manager to write the glowing narrative that attempts to differentiate your accomplishments. But very few narratives can overcome the stigma of being ranked 7 out of 7, even though you are in the topmost category. A little bit of statistical thinking can help here.

The people who are ranked below average try to emulate those who are ranked above average or otherwise change what they are doing to get a better rating or to improve. Because about half the people are trying to change to become above average, the variability of the outcomes of the organization can increase to twice what it would be if they would have just continued what they were doing. This is another way the reality of overcontrol can contribute to waste. Obviously, businesses cannot consistently meet their customers' needs with a system that fosters greater variability. Even if those below average do not try to change, they may be devastated by the stigma of being below average. Until they recover from that shock, their productivity and quality will suffer. We cannot do business today with that kind of waste.

Another factor which contributes to increased variability is indirectly caused by the use of management-by-exception. If you really stop to think about Dr. Deming's philosophy, management-by-exception should be seriously questioned. The exceptions that are brought to management's attention, typically are, special cases and could be more appropriately handled by the local process managers. Your job as management should be to work on the system of common causes. Myron Tribus, director of the Center for Advanced Engineering Studies at MIT, has perceptively stated that management works on the system, its people work in the system. Because exceptions are usually problems or other crises, the opportunity to give or receive positive feedback is generally not afforded to people. This, coupled with the fact that most traditional appraisal systems provide for but one formal evaluation session per year, is rightfully being questioned. The recommendation to take every opportunity to give positive feedback, however, might lead to unwanted variability. This is because management does not understand the difference between special and common causes of variability. They are treating each point as if it were a special cause. This results in the employee reacting to every piece of feedback with the inevitable increased variability stemming from overcontrol (see Chapter 3).

Some managers, in doing their best, have emphasized the customer feedback loop by recognizing an employee of the month, quarter or year, with an award which supposedly rewards positive accomplishments. In fact, it only increases the variability of performance of the organization. This is because those that did not win the award in the particular period mistakenly assume that it was process feedback and try to adjust their actions to emulate the person that did win. The reality and the waste of overcontrol strikes again. Criteria for the award typically include fewest mistakes or complaints, most votes from customers, and highest sales or volume of output for the particular period of time. These systems are usually lotteries, and the awards are actually distributed by chance. Consider this example:

You are a manager with eight employees reporting directly to you. They have essentially the same responsibilities, and in the past quarter they have recorded the following number of mistakes.

PERIOD	1	2	3	4	5	6	7	8	9	10	11	12	TOTAL
EMPLOYEE													
A	1	0	1	1	1	0	1	1	0	0	1	1	8
B	0	1	0	2	0	1	0	1	0	0	0	1	6
C	1	0	1	3	0	1	2	2	1	0	0	1	12
D	0	0	0	0	0	0	0	0	0	0	0	2	2
E	0	0	0	1	1	0	1	3	2	0	1	2	11
F	0	0	3	1	1	1	1	1	0	1	1	1	11
G	0	0	0	0	0	1	1	2	0	0	1	2	7
H	0	0	0	0	2	2	1	0	0	0	1	1	7
TOTAL	2	1	5	8	5	6	7	10	3	1	5	11	64

Figure 5-4

The Employee-of-the-Quarter award goes to employee D because he had the fewest mistakes this month. But what about next quarter? If there were many opportunities to make a mistake but only a small chance of making one at any one time, some simple calculations will show that all of the employees belong to the same system. And the variability of that system accounts for the results of employee C and employee D as well as all of those in between. Next quarter, someone else will take his turn in this lottery.

Rosabeth Moss Kanter observed that random reinforcement—an uncertain, apparently senseless cycle of rewards not clearly linked to behavior—provokes more anxiety than does negative reinforcement.[24]

The performance appraisal system confounds the people with the other resources. As you saw in Chapter 3, people are just one input to a process. Other inputs include the methods, environment, equipment, and materials. The main assumption in rewarding or punishing people is that they are solely responsible for the results of the process. Yet we know that the outcomes are the result of blending all of the inputs. Certainly we see differences in accomplishments, but are those differences due to the system or the individual? I have had the opportunity of talking to quite a few senior executives in both government and industry, and many of them relate stories of how they were able to ride the system at one time or another during their career. At those times, other inputs had a greater effect on the outcome than they did. Others who followed in that position were not as fortunate. The system overshadowed their best efforts and they did not meet their objectives. Former General Motors Chairman R. C. Gerstenberg said of even his job, "I am like an ant on the front of a log heading downstream toward a treacherous bend and all I can do is stick my foot in the water to try to steer us clear and yell 'whoa you SOB whoa' ".[25]

The performance appraisal system focuses on the short term. Short term is a relative term. It varies by industry and by discipline within industry. It ranges from hourly in a production environment to years in a research environment. Most senior management focuses on 90 days. Lee Iacocca swears by his quarterly reviews[26], while others swear at them. I certainly do not have his experience, but 40 quarters does not 10 years make. At least not in this new economic age. Nevertheless, senior management is often evaluated on short-term results.

> In theory, management and shareholders have a common interest in increasing their company's efficiency and profitability. In practice, as every investor knows, their interests often diverge. Take the case of a company that ties management compensation to some financial measure, such as earnings per share. Managers will be tempted—and many will succumb to the temptation—to take short-term steps to drive up earnings by putting off a needed investment in a new plant, say, or by resorting to some accounting gimmick.[27]

There are external pressures on management to be short-term oriented as we saw in Chapter 1 with ITT. The reason that the money managers reacted to the cut in dividends was that they are evaluated on the returns of their portfolios quarterly.

Money managers themselves are increasingly judged on their quarterly results. Now that computers tote up each trade and track overall fund returns, even their weekly and daily results can be tallied and compared with those of their peers. Because they are judged on their short-term performance, money managers seek the highest yield in the shortest time.[28]

More than a few managers have "succeeded" in a system which demands profits at all costs. They have shown profits by eliminating or otherwise reducing maintenance or research or testing or a myriad of other investments in the future.

I have seen a division manager meet his objectives, but in the process severely compromise his or his successor's chances of any real improvements. One of his plants was performing exceedingly well compared to the agreed-upon budget. Morale was high. There was even a spirit of initiative to experiment with ideas for improvement because even if they failed, they would still meet their budget. Another plant was not as fortunate. They were over budget. Despite repeated assurances to the contrary, the division manager had the well-performing plant's savings booked by finance. Both budget and headcount were reduced and the well-performing plant was expected to save at least the equivalent amount next year. Do you think that the plant will ever again be as open with their projected savings? Do you think that they will cooperate since they were penalized for their excellence? You cannot balance your budget in the short term by expensing people, at least not more than once.

In another oft-repeated scene, a new division manager comes in and replaces all of the people in key positions with trusted associates. Why did he do this? He was expected to show results within one year, maybe two. He increased his chances of getting these short-term results by having people around him who already know how he thinks and what he wants. He got these short-term gains at the long-term expense of people. The good ones who are not fired will look for employment elsewhere. But that is another management team's problem, isn't it? This one will be milking another organization.

The auto industry's focus on the short term is showcased in the 10-day sales report. The obvious object of this report is to reassure the country and

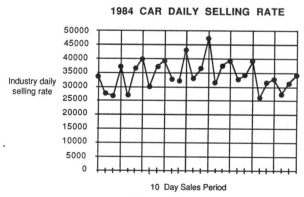

1984 CAR DAILY SELLING RATE

Industry daily selling rate (y-axis)

10 Day Sales Period

Figure 5-5

the money managers as well as the companies' managers that the metal is moving to the customer. The waste is not as obvious, but can be very expensive. The external pressures to show sales performance has led internal management to track sales daily. Again, for the best of reasons, management wants to be sure that there will be no surprises every ten days. It is this micro-management mentality which results in overcontrol of the system and costly waste.

If we look at the first nine months in 1984, we see an obvious pattern in the system. The last 10-day period in every month has the highest daily selling rate. The first 10-day period in every month has the lowest daily selling rate. People are borrowing from the first ten days to make their program objectives and look good for the month. This is accomplished by cascading the cajoling from Detroit to the districts, the districts to the zones, and the zones to the dealers. Valuable manpower is spent playing the system instead of meeting customers' needs. But the waste is not just manpower. Three times a month the vast communications systems are overloaded with messages to move the merchandise. It is no coincidence that those three days are just before the 10-day sales reports are due. If you size your communications system for those peak days, or have to delay other communications traffic, you are wasting resources which otherwise could be used to compete in world markets.

I've stated what is wrong with present appraisal systems; now I want to address the issue of what a system would look like that was supportive of continuing improvement. Dr. Deming has always said that it is management's sacred responsibility to counsel and develop its people. Unfortunately, company appraisal systems and bureaucracies have gotten in the way, and it is with these systems that Dr. Deming takes objection. The principal purposes of an appraisal and development system should be to nurture and sustain individual employee contributions to the continuous improvement of the organization as a team and to provide an assessment or evaluation of performance for the employee and management. The system must be based on a deep regard for people and recognize that employees are the organization's most important resource. The system should contribute to the development and motivation of all employees. This tenet will require a continuous effort in counseling, coaching and honest, open communications between the employee and the supervisor, supported by opportunities for enhancement of professional, managerial, and interpersonal skills.

A proposal that fosters teamwork. The definition of a process given in Chapter 3 is easy to understand in the context of manufacturing. In fact, those kinds of processes are the only ones which people typically associate as being processes. What is more difficult to understand is the myriad of other business processes, the control and reduction of variability, which are vital to future competitiveness. Such processes include the managing of accounts receivable, the control of engineering drawings, managing customer feedback, and even developing group objectives. The process of developing group objectives is just as much a process as grinding camshafts or processing accounts receivable. And it might be more important because through it we can begin to build the teamwork needed to meet our other customers' needs.

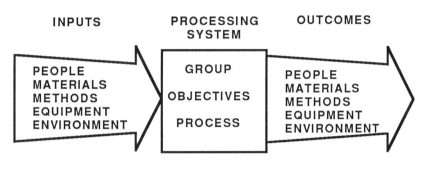

Figure 5-6

We can better understand the process by looking at its three main parts:
- The outcomes
- The process
- The inputs

Outcomes. The first step is to define the outcomes. For the process of developing group objectives the outcome is, of course, group objectives. Why are they so important? Because they can form the bond necessary to get people from differing departments and organizations to work as a team in meeting their customers' needs. Two words are important here. The first is group. Although I am defining more than one person as a group, the focus should be on those outside one's immediate organization. Teamwork among one's own organization is also important, but it can be facilitated within the confines of the organization. Group objectives, on the other hand, are necessary to coalesce people having no immediate mutual manager. The second word is objectives. And it is not what you might think. The emphasis should be on the method or process used to meet your customers' needs and not on the attainment of some intermediate result. As soon as you put a number on an objective, it will be self limiting (see Chapter 9). On a recent trip to Japan, I talked with some Deming Medal-winning companies about their evaluation systems. Although each was different (I knew that before I started), there was a common thread. And that was that for raises and bonuses; the prime criterion was performance (whatever that means). But for promotions, however, the prime criterion was harmony or promoting team-work. I think this balance is critical in any organization. You do not get ahead by crawling all over people. You get ahead by fostering teamwork. That really is a manager's prime responsibility; to develop and direct a group of people so that they may meet their customers' needs more efficiently than if they worked alone—in other words, synergy.

Process. The process of developing group objectives is best shown using a process flow diagram (see Chapter 11). The process is composed of four subprocesses.

Identify your customers' needs and operationally define their critical characteristics. For instance, an employee in Operation 20 might be machining gear blanks which are then hobbed in Operation 30. The customer in this case is Operation 30. The employee in Operation 20 should talk to his counterpart in Operation 30 to find out which characteristics are critical to Operation 30 and how Operation 20 might better meet his needs. (Obviously, all of this is constrained by the needs of the ultimate customer.) After talking, they agree that the outside diameter (O.D.) of the blank is a critical characteristic and is one that Operation 20 can influence.

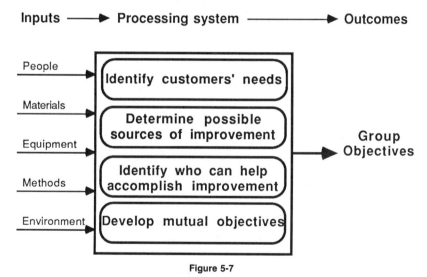

Figure 5-7

Operation 20 must *determine the possible sources of improvement* to meet those needs. Once the critical characteristics are agreed upon, the employee in Operation 20 should construct a cause and effect diagram as an aid to identifying the resources or inputs contributing to the variability of the O.D. of the gear blank. A review of these sources of variability reveals that tools are a very important resource to control.

CAUSE AND EFFECT DIAGRAM

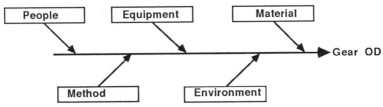

Figure 5-8

Determine who can help accomplish the improvement. Within any company, several organizations affect the variability of the tools: purchasing, engineering, quality control, and the tool room, to name a few. These are obvious, but there may be others which are not so obvious.

Meet with them (departmental units) to develop mutual objectives which lead to satisfying your customers' needs. The objective strategy meeting and ultimate consensus on what your mutual objectives should be is essential. A unilateral objective on Operation 20's part is not as effective as a mutually agreed upon objective between Operation 20 and purchasing.

Inputs. In order to improve any of the subprocesses, we must understand the sources of variability which affect the process. These sources of variability can come from the process inputs. This really is a listing of the people, equipment, materials, methods, and environment that blend in the process of developing group objectives.

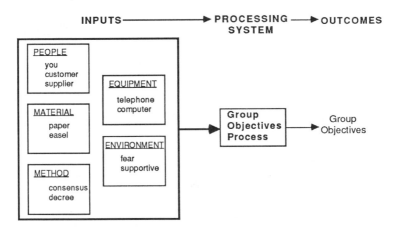

Figure 5-9

The people resource is obvious. By identifying early on your customers and suppliers as well as any other relevant people resource, you have formed the basis for teamwork when it is needed. Another dominant resource is the environment. Will the culture permit cooperation and teamwork, or is there fear and excessive internal competition? There is also a variety of methods which could be used to develop group objectives. They could be established by the first manager common to both organizations. They could be set by the dominant manager or organization. They could be agreed upon by consensus. Whatever the method, the ultimate goal is to continually improve the competitiveness of the organization.

It occurs to me that if teamwork is so important, and it is, then we should step out of the dark ages in our team selection process. It is certainly a step in the right direction to choose people based on their teamwork characteristics as well as their other technical expertise. But our interview process still looks at one person at a time. Now, we might interview them in quick succession, or have them interviewed by a number of people, but we do not bring in a group to be interviewed as a prospective team member. We need to experiment with the people to determine the various interactions necessary to get the best synergism. This is something that cannot be determined if you interview them one at a time. They might all pass your criteria for team players, but put them all together and the results might not be as good as you would have gotten with a different mix of people because of the interactions. Now, there are some relatively simple experimental methods (see Chapter 11) that will aid in selecting the best blend of people for the team. I think there is a great opportunity in this human resources area for improvement with the addition of some statistical thinking.

A proposal that fosters excellence.

We know that mediocrity is the result when fear of failure permeates an organization. This is due to the attributes-type appraisal system which focuses singlemindedly on the objective. You either meet the objective, or you do not meet it. As with any process, if you focus on the outcome, you will not be competitive in this new economic age. You must focus on the process if you are to continually improve your ability to meet your customers' needs and expectations. You must focus on the process if you are to really pursue excellence.

Lloyd Nelson, Director of Statistical Methods at Nashua Corporation, tells of a manager who agreed to a 5 percent savings the next year. When asked by what method will he get the savings, he answered that he had not thought of that. To which Dr. Nelson replied that if you can save 5 percent without a method, why didn't you do it this year? You must have been goofing off.

A lot of managers will say, "Of course we have methods. Of course we have a plan to meet our objectives." Unfortunately, many of these plans are backed into to support or justify the objectives. Management must be very adept at this game to survive.

One strategy to make the transition from attributes outcomes to managing process variables is to specify a range of outcomes instead of a go/no-go threshold. This way, you can begin to avoid the games people play to come in exactly on or just a bit over the objective. Granted, you still may have people stopping or slowing down once they are in the established range of outcomes. But if your emphasis is upstream on the process, only excellence will follow.

A proposal that fosters consistency.

The prime cause for increasing variability is management's not understanding it in the first place. An example here should help.

You are a manager with nine employees reporting directly to you. (You have a full span of control.) They have essentially the same responsibilities and in the past year they have recorded the following number of mistakes. The types of mistakes are purposefully omitted because of the broad applicability of this example. They could be bookkeeping errors, engineering drawing mistakes, assembly worker errors, etc. The only restriction is that there were many opportunities to make a mistake, but only a small chance of making one particular mistake at any one time.

Employee	Number of Mistakes
1	10
2	15
3	11
4	4
5	17
6	23
7	11
8	12
9	10

It is time for evaluations and merit raise recommendations. Who do you reward? Who do you penalize? (For the purposes of this example, the other qualitative measures are roughly the same for all employees.)

Some solutions follow.

Most managers will look to reward the employee who made the fewest mistakes. They will also frown on the one who made the most mistakes. The assumption is that those particular employees' performances are significantly different from the rest and are also a direct result of their individual abilities. A manager might analyze the performance of this employees by ranking them from least mistakes to most.

performance of his employees by ranking them from least mistakes to most.

Rank	Employee	Number of Mistakes
1	4	4
2	1	10
3	9	10
4	3	11
5	7	11
6	8	12
7	2	15
8	5	17
9	6	23

A more informed manager might wish to look at the data graphically.

Rank order

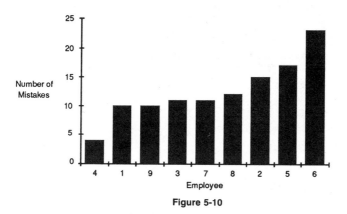

Figure 5-10

This is at least a start in the analysis of these data. Unfortunately, rank ordering does not indicate whether there is a significant difference between the numbers, and this is the assumption that we need to verify before we take action. We knew from the start that one of the nine employees would be in the top 11 percent and one would be in the bottom 11 percent ($1/9 = 11.11\%$). We knew that before we gathered any data. What we need to know is whether or not the top or bottom 11 percent are part of the system, and if they are not, and thus in need of different treatment.

In this situation and, in fact, any time there is a count made of the number of occurrences of an event which had many opportunities to happen, but which was extremely unlikely to occur at any given opportunity and only one occurrence per any opportunity, and the area of opportunity is constant, and the occurrences are independent of one another, a control chart called a C-chart may be used to determine if all the occurrences came from the same system. The use of the tool is simple. First, calculate the average number of mistakes made by the employees involved. An arithmetic mean is calculated by adding the individual numbers and dividing their sum by the number of individual numbers.

$$(10 + 15 + 11 + 4 + 17 + 23 + 11 + 12 + 10)/9 = 12.56$$

Second, to estimate the standard deviation, calculate the square root of the average.

$$\sqrt{12.56} = 3.54$$

We know that if the actual data are between the average plus and minus three standard deviations, the process is predictable, it is in statistical control. When this is the case, management is responsible for improvement because the system or process is doing the best it can, given the blending of resources at that point. If a point is outside the control limits, this indicates that someone is not operating in the same system as everyone else. In this example, the control limits are 23.19 for the upper control limit and 1.93 for the lower control limit. The following control chart shows that all of the employees reporting to you are operating under the same system or process because there is no indication of special causes of variation.

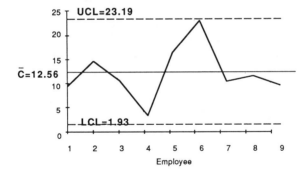

Figure 5-11

From the viewpoint of the manager, no one employee's performance is that much different than anyone else's. To reward or penalize based on relative ranking would be detrimental, as they are all performing within the system that you are managing. Any improvement must come from the system, which is your responsibility. You must change or reblend the resources.

What if Employee number 6 made 24 mistakes during the past year instead of 23? Well, the chart would look like this, with the average number of mistakes equal to 12.67 and the upper control limit equal to 23.35, and the lower control limit equal to 1.99.

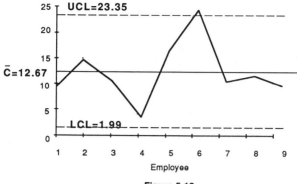

Figure 5-12

You can see right away that Employee 6 is not within the calculated control limits. This means that you as a manager do not have a predictable system and that, at the very least, Employee 6 is operating at a level sufficiently different from the rest of the employees to warrant your attention.

One of the first things that I would do is to find out whether the remaining eight employees are operating as a predictable system. Is their performance in a state of statistical control? You can do this by eliminating Employee 6 from the calculations and recalculating the average number of mistakes as well as the upper and lower control limits. (Remember that this recalculation does not reflect reality unless you identify and remove the source of the special cause.) You can see in this next control chart that the C bar (average number of mistakes) equals 11.25, which means that the upper control limit is 21.31 and the lower control limit is 1.19. The data of the process are telling us that the remaining eight employees are all part of the same system. Their improvement is up to you, their manager, to change or reblend the resources.

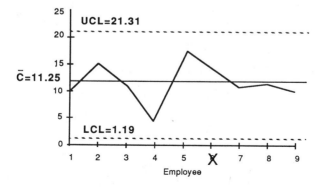

Figure 5-13

If another employee were outside the recalculated control limits, I would exclude this point and recalculate until there was an indication of a system of a group of employees. Then I would look at the excluded data to see if they form a system together. But in this example, there is only one excluded point. Before you, the manager, can take appropriate action, you must determine whether Employee 6 just by chance made 24 mistakes or this level will likely continue.

To do this, you need to look at the performance of Employee 6 over time. If the data were in a state of statistical control at a particular level, you would know that the level will continue if the input of Employee 6 remains essentially the same.

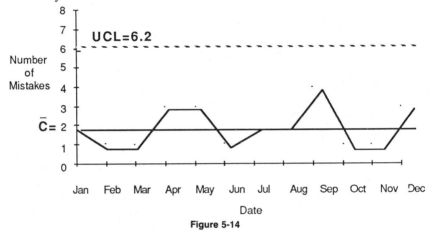

Figure 5-14

We see that employee 6 makes an average number of 2 mistakes per month and is in control at that level. This means that the employee will make predictably, on the average, 24 mistakes per year. If this is not satisfactory, and it shouldn't be because 1) you want people to improve and 2) the employee was outside the system on the "bad" side, then you as a manager should look to retraining the employee on a different job because further training on the current job would be fruitless. That is, unless his perception of the current assignment is sufficiently changed to permit training to be effective.

A worker who is in a state of control but whose work is unsatisfactory presents a problem. It is usually uneconomical to try to retrain him on the same job. It is more economical to put him into a new job in which the training may be more expert than it was in his present job.[2]

A person is in a state of statistical control at an unacceptable level. Dr. Deming has seen time and time again that further training in the same job does not result in improvement.

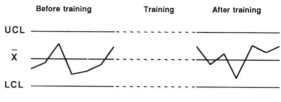

Figure 5-15

On the other hand, if the data were not in statistical control, then, depending on the reason for the special cause(s), the high level might be temporary.

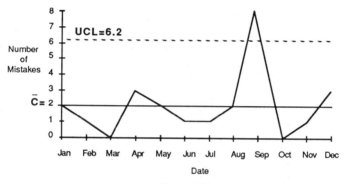

Figure 5-16

The reason for the unusually high number of mistakes in September might have been due to illness or some other temporary special cause. Unless it is found and corrected, however, it could come back to affect Employee 6's performance again.

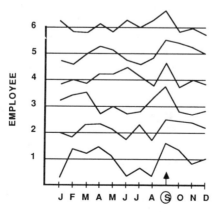

Figure 5-17

The cause for the unusually high number of mistakes in September might have been bad incoming material which affected all the employees. You won't know unless you look at the data for the rest of the employees over time as you did with Employee 6.

The purpose of the above example is to show that you need to understand variability if you are to get consistency. Rewarding those that make the fewest mistakes and penalizing those that make the most will increase the variability of your system, if you even have one.

Even though many evaluation systems have about ten rating categories, only about three or four of them are ever really used. What I am proposing reflects this reality as well as having a basis in statistical theory. I am proposing a rating method which recognizes the fact that most people should be performing within a system. By this I mean that from the perspective of the manager, his people are in statistical control. If you are performing within a system, there can be no further distinction of being above or below average or the top or bottom 1 percent. The same system that produced the top 10 percent produced the bottom 10 percent. The next time you measure, the position might be reversed. The rating system would reflect the fact that that there are only three possibilities of position: outside the system on the low side, in the system, and outside the system on the high side.

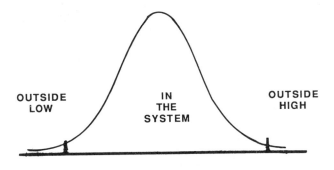

Figure 5-18

I don't wish to imply a normal distribution, but actual data show high in the middle and low on the ends. In any event, no more than 5 to 11 percent are outside the system (Chebyshev's theorem states that no matter what the distribution, the probability of an observation being outside of **3 standard deviations** is less than or equal to $1/3^2 = .11$. Camp and Meidell have observed that if the distribution has only one mode, and the **mode** is the same as the **arithmetic mean**, and if the observations continuously decline on both sides of the mode, then the probability of an observation being outside of **3 standard deviations** is less than or equal to $1/(2.25 \times 3^2) =$

.05. The rest are in the system. If you have the data, as you did in the previous example, then they will tell you if you have a system, who is in it and who is not. If you don't have the data, then the question is not who is ranked number one or last. The question is who is clearly not part of the system, recognizing that the system can exhibit quite a lot of variability. If no one is obviously outstanding on the high or low sides, then everyone belongs to the system. Merit raises can only make sense with this rating scheme. The only people eligible for a merit raise are those outstanding on the high side. The rest of the people in the system should evenly share the remaining monies set aside for reinvestment in the organization's most important resource, its people.

A fourth category may be applicable over time. If an employee shows improving or declining performance for seven consecutive periods, then that is an indication of a special cause, and the employee should be recognized as outstanding on the high or low side. The periods need not be in one-year increments. Business cycles and dynamics many times are on another periodicity. For example, auto industry sales people get an informal review every ten days, while researchers might not have tangible results for a few years.

Two questions are typically raised:

Doesn't the outside the system on the high side rating encourage individualism and destroy teamwork? Not if the criteria include teamwork. When this is the case, a person cannot be outside the system unless he excels in teamwork.

How would you distribute evenly the monies to the people rated in the system? One way is similar to keeping score at the card game of bridge. You keep track of the accomplishments of the various teams that you are a member of, and when the monies are to be divided, you would get your share. Each team could allocate by consensus, shares similar to professional teams in the playoffs of sports. The shares could be equal or unequal, depending on the decision of the team.

Will these suggested changes work? Only time will tell. Ford Motor Company is piloting some of the system I just described. Preliminary results are encouraging, although people are having difficulty understanding the benefits of the rating scheme. The important thing to remember is that management has a responsibility to coach, counsel and develop its people. If the system stands in the way of that responsibility, then it must be changed. What it must be changed to will require further experimentation by organizations willing to innovate, willing to improve.

2. Daily Production Reports.

Another inhibitor to continuing improvement is rather innocuous. It takes the form of the daily production report. These seemingly informative documents quantify the number of whatever is produced the previous day and many also give measures of productivity. What is not realized by management is that they place undo pressure for sheer quantity. The crux of the problem with this report is also symptomatic of other management reports in that its distribution is the prime inhibitor. Certainly someone must manage by the day. Someone must manage by the hour. And someone must manage by the decade. The distribution of these reports would indicate that everyone is managing by the hour. These reports go daily up the chain of command to the highest levels. If production is down one day, there had better be an explanation. Because of the distribution of the reports, the phone calls cascade down from the front office to the plant manager and beyond. The plant manager's reaction to the system is understandable and predictable. He has learned to survive. In my travels I have observed that:

1.) He is hoping that if something is going to go wrong, it will do so early in the morning so that he will be able to patch the problem and have the rest of the day to catch his production quota. The system forces short-term patches instead of long-lasting solutions. (I have seen some companies force plant managers to call in hourly production figures to corporate headquarters, the ultimate in short-term, quantity oriented, micromanagement, overcontrol.)

2.) He typically has salted away some production for a day when he needs it to make his quota. Likewise, first line supervisors will bank output to protect their hourly shortfalls. They are saving for preholiday inefficiencies, end-of-day "cleanup time", and other causes of production shortfall. The waste is obvious. The pressure on quantity compromises quality as well as productivity.

3.) He will spend valuable creative thinking time coming up with explanations for the variance in his daily quota. This is waste because he should be using his creative energies trying to meet his customers' needs.

4.) He might be lucky enough to have an understanding controller who realizes that the front office gets all exercized when they see all that variability and smoothes the figures to avoid the unnecessary worry at the top. One over-used way to play with the numbers is to mark it "shipped" if it helps the plant numbers.

Much of the above waste can be eliminated by giving the appropriate wheel base to the plant manger (or any other manager) to recover from the day-to-day problems that will occur. One way to mitigate the daily pressure is to distribute the five or six daily reports to upper management weekly instead of daily. The reason for this recommendation, and not just giving management weekly aggregated numbers, revolves around management's solemn obligation to develop their people. If they use the information their people used to make decisions, they then get the opportunity to say "I see the basis for your decision, here is how I would have made it given this data." You can't do that if you are looking at aggregated data. Besides, someone or some computer has to aggregate it, and that costs money. Don't waste resources, especially human resources. Your customer can't afford it.

Speaking of waste, the most wasted resource in industry is management. They may think that they are applying their expertise and knowledge, but it is wasted because they are effectively isolated from much of the reality of business. Some people are paid to manage by the decade, others are paid to manage by the hour. We are all not paid to manage by the hour. Nevertheless, many top managers signal that they want to manage by the hour by the reporting systems they set up. Because of the way they treated bad news in the past, they will insure that they will only see good news. Through killing the messenger they guarantee that the information passed up to them will be filtered and censored to minimize their fear-inducing reaction.

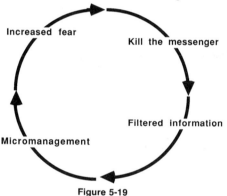

Figure 5-19

Management is not dumb. They realize that the information they receive is filtered and censored. So they try to get to the source of the information by going around their valuable middle management. They do this either directly or through their computerized information systems. In either case, this micromanagement further instills fear in the organization and the vicious circle continues. All because of the way management reacts to data. All because management quickly forgets the games they played when they were in their subordinate's positions.

3. Financial Management System.

The financial management system can also be an inhibitor to continuing improvement. It can be too restrictive and focus on the short term. By too restrictive, I mean that management does not have the flexibility to trade off resources, because in some corporate cultures, if you miss one line item in the budget, you have failed. One way to give management flexibility is to give them a budget with only two of the three parameters of any business:

- Revenue
- Cost
- Profit

Given the two parameters, the third is determined. They then have the flexibility to manage their resources and not play games with specific budget line items. But even specifying these major business parameters might be stifling another very necessary business function, and that is communication. When budget figures are given, it can be very easy to turn within your own organization to meet the prescribed budget. But what happens when no one gives you the figures? In an environment of continuing improvement, you are forced to talk to others outside your organization to see how your plans will affect and will be affected by others. It forces communication to take place.

By focusing on the short term, I mean the emphasis on "What have you done for me this quarter or this year?" Anyone can show a profit if he cuts out maintenance or training or R&D or any of a number of longer-range investments.

The managing of labor and overhead accounts often is a time sink for creative bookkeeping. The system can force these games if you need to conduct maintenance and you haven't worked the direct labor yet. In the longer term, one can show headcount savings or reduction by outsourcing the job whether it be engineering, accounting, manufacturing, etc. It may increase the total cost, but you have reduced your all important labor and overhead expenses. You aren't fooling anyone, and you are especially not fooling the customer.

Cost of Quality

A lot of things are fashionable these days: Statistical Process Control (SPC); Just-in-Time (inventory policy) (JIT); Quality of Work Life (QWL); and Total Quality Control (TQC). Cost of quality is also one that is getting more than its share of attention. Consultants are coming out of the woodwork selling quality systems to management on the basis of reducing the cost of quality and thereby directly increasing the bottom line. "Think of all the additional product you would have to sell to put an equivalent dollar value in the profit column." Dr. Juran has astutely observed that the language of top management is dollars. These consultants then figure that by mentioning equivalent ROI's, this will get management's attention and investment in their quality cost system. One has to augment his existing financial system to measure the costs of controlling quality and the costs of failing to control it. Sounds great, doesn't it? And in fact, reducing cost while improving quality is what everyone must do in this new economic age. But beefing up one of the bigger inhibiting systems in the world is not the way to achieve it. What do I mean by this? Cost is composed of visible and invisible figures. Dr. Deming has said that if you manage your company on visible figures alone, you will soon have neither company nor visible figures to work with. Obviously, there is a lot of uncertainty in invisible figures. Who knows the cost of a dissatisfied customer or a satisfied employee? But let's take a close look at the visible ones, the ones that are so precisely reported. Even though all the columns and rows add up exactly, how did a figure get on the sheet? Whose cost estimate are you using? What are the facts? For that matter, what is a fact? It, like history, is what somebody else wants to let you know.

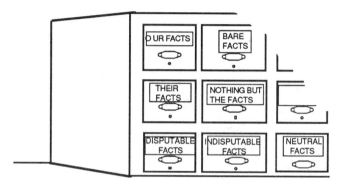

Figure 5-20

And if there is fear in the organization, your chance of knowing what really is behind a figure is very slim.

Some people will say that the intent of the financial management system is very good, it's just that the message sometimes gets fouled up when you carry it out, the supposition being that if only people would do as they were instructed, everything would be okay. This statement is actually the heart of the problem. There are a lot of systems that look good on paper. The real problem is to create a system that will result in the intent being carried out. Dr. Deming has said many times that the operational definition of any procedure is what you get when it is carried out, not what is written down on a piece of paper or what was nobly intended by the author. I am reminded of a quote from Rod McKuen "If you had listened hard enough, you might have heard what I meant to say." It is not good enough for the intent of financial planning figures to be a guideline for management when, in actuality, they are the law. It is not good enough to say that controllers are advisors when the burden of proof lies with line management. Unless they can prove enough cost effectiveness to make it over some internal hurdle rate or clearly show an immediate offset, they can't act. Some decisions are a clear "do it" or "don't do it". But many are pretty fuzzy and result in management either backing into the numbers or arguing with the controller, both of which waste valuable resources.

I observed in the beginning of this chapter that one of the big pressures on engineers in the auto industry is to reduce cost while maintaining performance. The science is refined to the point that some savings are accrued at $0.001 per car. Engineers would kill for a mere $50 per car. Just imagine what they could do to improve the car with $500. And yet, when the companies enter into a rebate war, they are giving away that much and more to try to sell the cars. Wouldn't it be better to engineer and build it into the car to begin with and get a premium on top of sticker price like the international competition is doing? The financial managment system somehow adjusts to crises such as responding to the competition's marketing initiative, or safety campaigns, or liability concerns. But it is very stingy when there is more time and less apparent urgency to address an opportunity.

The fault is not all with the financial community. In more than one instance, line management has rejected finance's proposals to change the system to make it more responsive to the operations' needs. The reason for the rejection has been that line management feels very secure in their ability to understand and manipulate the current system. They would be on unfamiliar ground with a new system.

Obviously, no organization can survive if they do not use a wide array of financial management tools. These tools can benefit from statistical thinking and the managers that use them can benefit by understanding that they are just tools, not the answers.

Chapter 6

Drive out fear, so that everyone may work effectively for the company. (Point 8)

I personally don't think that fear will ever be driven from the workplace. It is everywhere and comes in many forms. One of those forms can be helpful, especially in the beginning stages of a company's transition to continuing improvement. In the early days of Ford's transition, Don Petersen (then president, now chairman) would, in his visits to the operations, ask how they were doing on SPC. (He now knows that this is not the right question to ask, but more on that later.) The president of Ford Motor Company needs only ask a question once and you can be sure that every effort will be expended to give an answer. Our office telephone would predictably ring as he made his rounds. The queries were almost always the same, "Where can we learn more about SPC?" and "How can you help us?" Fear was part of the motivation, but we had a responsibility to follow up once the door was open. I looked on it as the lesser of evils. Fear is the antithesis of Dr. Deming's philosophies, but apathy and short-term myopia were an even bigger roadblock to learning about the other thirteen.

Fear is one of those highly leveraged qualities. You only need to kill a messenger once and word gets around. Everybody knows that one "Aw shit" wipes out twenty "atta boys". Dr. Deming has found that the removal or reduction of fear should be one of the first of his fourteen obligations which top management starts to implement, because it affects nine of his other points. Without an atmosphere of mutual respect, no statistically based management system will work, nor any other.

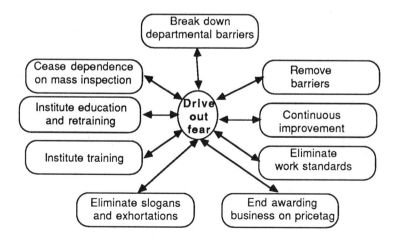

Figure 6-1

The waste due to fear is enormous. It is one of those invisible figures, however, and thus doesn't get management's immediate attention. Some of the following examples should help:

The CEO is presiding at a meeting. He raises his eybrows at a point in one of the presentations. In a fear-filled organization, that simple piece of body language results in man-months of wasteful staff action. They research every possible reason the CEO might have had to raise his eyebrows. Position papers and reports are written. Contingency plans are drawn. They do almost everything except to ask him what he meant by it. Had someone the courage to ask, he might have avoided much of the wasted human effort.

The vice president for sales is presiding at a meeting of his sales managers. They know full well that if any of them predicts an increase of less than 10 percent for the next year, he won't have a job there. It makes no difference whether he makes the predicted increase. They all must go through this wasteful ritual.

The COO is presiding at a meeting of his direct reports. In a fear-filled organization, everyone brings in reams of backup material defying each other to ask a question that he cannot answer. It costs a lot of money and time to brief these people. It costs a lot less to be able to say "I'll find out, sir." In this kind of fear-filled atmosphere, glibness is treated as a short term asset when, in reality, it is a long-term liability. There is real waste when you are always expected to have an answer.

In many companies, fear aids communication. It is the wrong kind of communication, but at least the people are talking to one another. The communication takes place prior to talking to a superior. It takes the form of "If you don't mess in my nest, I won't mess in yours." And it takes some real communication to keep the top management thinking that their organization is doing fine and has the necessary altruism and teamwork necessary to succeed in the marketplace. Unfortunately, this is just another example of the ways in which top management is given a filtered view of what is really going on in their organizations.

An executive vice president is visiting an operating facility. In his carefully orchestrated visit, he sees only what they wish him to see. No problems, just bright smiling faces, all in their places. During one such dog and pony show, a plant manager was showing off several median charts used to help manage his people's processes. The partially enlightened EVP wanted to know why they were using median charts and not X bar and R charts. (He had never heard of median charts.) Within a week, only X bar and R charts were being used in his plants. Anything to keep him happy. He exhibited a common characteristic of people learning about a single statistical method—if the only tool you have is a hammer, it is surprising how many things start looking like a nail.

A partially enlightened plant manager has made it clear that he wants all of his processes in statistical control. With a combination of fear and ignorance, his people are able to bring virtually every process into statistical control. But they do this by taking five samples randomly per shift. Why five? Why randomly throughout the shift? Because they observed that the five pieces distributed over the shift masks most possibilities to discover a special cause. It in effect numbs the process so that it doesn't hurt from the pain of being out of control. A competent person can construct a sampling plan that will show any process to be in statistical control. But he would not advocate using it, because a competent statistician wants to help people improve. The state of statistical control must not be viewed as an end in itself. It is only a very necessary building block in the road to continuing improvement.

Dr. Deming has recently observed that fear of knowledge is pervasive in many levels of management. Some managers won't come to class because they don't want to appear ignorant. Some are too close to retirement to have any motivation to learn. Some are too steeped in their "superstitious learning" to change. Some fear the added responsibility that the new knowledge entails. Whatever their reasons, the result is reduced competitiveness because of management's sluggish response to change. One of the most important lessons that I have learned from Dr. Deming's example is that you must continue to improve; you must never stop learning. You are never too smart or too old or too important. I recently ran across the following quote:

Anyone who stops learning is old, whether at twenty or eighty. Anyone who keeps learning stays young. The greatest thing in life is to keep your mind young.

Henry Ford said that many decades ago. A pretty good challenge for managers, I'd say.

Chapter 7

Break down barriers between departments. People in research, design, sales, and production must work as a team to foresee problems of production and in use that may be encountered with the product or service. (Point 9)

Point 9 is closely aligned with Point 8 - Drive out fear. It also is a necessary but not sufficient condition of company-wide quality control. I talked about inhibitors to teamwork and ways to foster teamwork in Chapter 5, so I need not further discuss them here. I will, however, expand on a topic introduced in Chapter 1, and that is operationally defining the customers' critical characteristics throughout your entire organization. The Japanese have further developed this point of Dr. Deming's through the process known to many companies as "Quality Function Deployment".

The voice of the customer is deployed to all concerned by detailed tables known as K-K Tables or Koe-Kikaku Tables. (Koe means voice and kikaku means planning.) The following is excerpted from an excellent paper by Don Clausing of Xerox.

Figure 7-1 is a simple example for a sunroof. The required quality at the left is the customer requirement. In this simple example, there are two primary requirements:

- Rain should not leak into the sunroof.
- The sunroof should be capable of being opened and closed comfortably.

As indicated, the primary customer requirements are subdivided into secondary requirements. In actual practice, these are then usually further subdivided into tertiary requirements. In the real application of the quality planning chart, there are typically twenty to thirty tertiary customer requirements. Each row represents a customer requirement. Each column represents a planning requirement. The customer requirements are deployed into the planning requirements as shown by line number 1. The ability to comfortably operate the sunroof, which is a customer requirement, is deployed into the planning requirement of an important aspect of operability. In this simple example, it may seem that operability and comfortable use of the sunroof are just slightly different words for the same attribute. However, in actual practice, there is a much more clear distinction between the viewpoint of the customer and the viewpoint of the planners of the product.

The rows can be followed completely across the diagram to find additional information about the customer requirements. For example, line number 2 shows that a particular customer requirement is a strongly desired item, B-1. Further to the right shows the existing

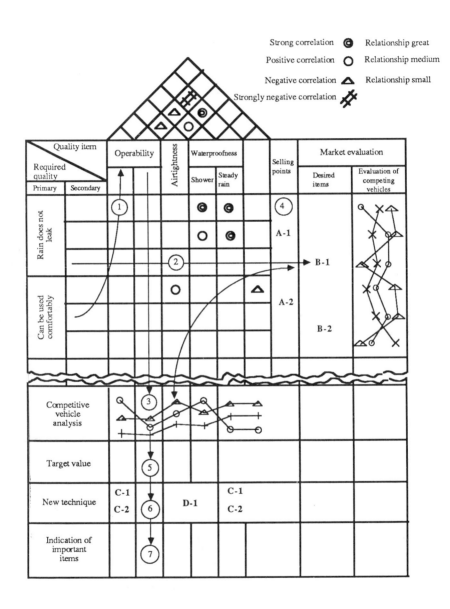

Figure 7-1

customer perception of three competitive products with respect to this particular customer requirement.

Following the columns downward, we find more information about planning requirements. At position number 3 we find an evaluation of the three competitive products in terms of one specific planning requirement. Thus, we see that the competitive evaluation is done both with respect to the rows, i.e., customer requirements, and the columns, i.e., planning requirements. As shown by the curved dashed line, one would of course wish to compare these two types of competitive evaluation. Extending further downward along a column, we find that at position 5 is listed the target value for the particular planning requirement. At position 6 is listed any new technique that will have to be employed to achieve this particular item that will be needed to achieve this planning requirement. This might be a major capital investment. In considering the customers' requirements, we follow the rows across to the column listed as Selling Points, and find as an example at position 4 a customer requirement which, if met in a creative and highly satisfactory way, would achieve a major selling point that the sales force could use to sell the product effectively.

The triangular section at the top of the chart displays the correlation among different planning requirements. For example, there is strong negative correlation between waterproofness against a steady rain and an important aspect of operability. This is common sense. We could easily achieve waterproofness against a steady rain by bolting the sunroof closed, but that would certainly make opening and closing the sunroof rather difficult. The strongly negative correlation mark indicates two conflicting requirements. Therefore, these requirements call for special attention to assure that both of the conflicting requirements will be met by the design.[29]

The rest of the world is not without its systems, too. Ford Motor Company uses a Design Approval Process (DAP)[30] which depends on the cooperation of many diverse organizations including the following:

Design Staff
Controller's Office
Sales and Marketing
Timing and Control
Advance Product Planning
Vehicle Engineering Office
Body and Assembly Purchasing
Body and Assembly Manufacturing
Powertrain and Chassis Operations
Product Planning

Diversified Products Operations (Glass, Plastic, Steel, Climate Control), etc.

Both systems look good on paper. Both are fostering the cooperation between departments. Both are trying to meet customers' needs. The trick is in the execution of the process. And here, there is no general remedy. There is no substitute for knowledge. There is no substitute for knowing your processes and improving on them. I want to make a point here, and it is that we do not need to rush out and make a wholesale replacement of our existing systems with Japanese systems. We can learn from them, but we cannot quickly "install" anything of worth.

I will make another observation. Although many systems look good on paper, employees are so deluged with other add-on "programs" that things can slip through the cracks. The systems are complied with as the exception and not as the rule. If the organization is audited, they will, just before the audit, turn multitudes of resources on the paperwork. When the auditors go away, it is back to business as usual, which is preparing for another audit in another area. It is hard to really break down barriers if you are constantly sending in the police. Even if you call them consultants or assistants, it is what they do that counts.

I have observed that major organizations (that is, big enough to be multidisciplinary) have departments or assignments which are fun and challenging. I remember when I worked in consulting firms, the fun and creative genius that was put into the "hunt", the proposal writing. Once you won, you would go off on another hunt, while the mundane business of performing the contract was many times someone else's worry. There is that same kind of cliquish challenge among design engineers, research and development scientists, strategic planning, automobile launch teams, and any of the other recognized assignments of innovation and visible problem solving. The obvious challenge is to get everyone involved in the innovation, everyone recognizing that they each have something to contribute and they can do so in an atmosphere of mutual respect. I think that operationally defining the ultimate customers' needs and expectations so that everyone understands how he contributes to the success of the organization is a solid step to breaking down barriers between departments.

Chapter 8

Eliminate slogans, exhortations, and targets for the work force that ask for zero defects and new levels of productivity. (Point 10)

O Gott, Ich bitt
Bewahr mein tritt
So fall Ich nitt

O God, I beg
Guide my step
So I do not fall

Certainly this is not the first slogan or exhortation, but it is the oldest one I have seen. It came from Burg Gutenfels on the Rhine river. This 13th century castle had this slogan inscribed in an extremely rickety staircase. The original owners evidently felt that some divine guidance would help them as they traversed those treacherous steps.

Dr. Deming tells of a modern-day exhortation that says "Safety is your responsibility". This sign was posted on some factory stairs without a railing which were in bad repair. Is safety solely the responsibility of the individual? Definitely not. Many times other resources in the system dominate and overshadow the individual's contribution to the outcome.

Certainly motivation and personal awareness are contributors to limiting the variability of the people in a process. But they are no substitute for training. They are no substitute for knowledge of the process. They are no substitute for the tools and methods necessary to help manage the process. Many managers know this, but still hedge their bets on the chance that their people really want and need these slogans and exhortations to do their work. The fact is that their money would be better spent on changing management systems so that their people could improve.

State-of-the-art electronics has added a new dimension to slogans and exhortations. That new dimension is overcontrol. I have seen computer driven signs in plants flashing the latest accident or production status and urging the workers to do better or surpass the latest figures. The obvious result of the use of this technology is greater variability and frustration.

Chapter 9

Eliminate work standards (quotas) on the factory floor. Substitute leadership. Eliminate management by objective. Eliminate management by numbers, numerical goals. Substitute leadership. (Point 11)

In typically Japanese fashion, NUMMI's Fremont plant will have an extremely slow startup. In the first few weeks, the sole line ran only an hour or two a day. It will take the better part of six to nine months before full production is reached; extensive training will take place during this time.[31]

Many people in management would say that the above example is bad business, that with all the machinery installed, they have yet to begin to generate a return on their assets. What these managers do not understand is that machinery is but one resource in a process. Dr. Deming would say that even though the plant is built, they have not yet fully invested in their most important asset, and that is their people. The employees in the plant must be trained. They must learn to work with the other resources, and this takes time. Thus, the plant is not completely built until all the resources are ready. The bodies may be there, but the people are not. If we compare the two approaches, we see one coming up quickly to just under the standard and remaining there for the duration of the life-cycle of the process. The other approach moves slowly to the standard, but continues past it over the duration of the life-cycle of the process.

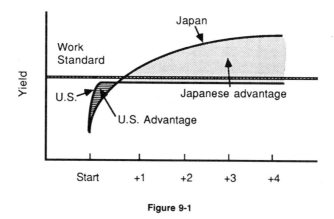

Figure 9-1

So although the U.S. approach might have an early advantage in productivity, the Deming approach, as seen through Japanese performance, might end up with more productivity throughout the life-cycle. Work standards tend to cap the amount of improvement that can be achieved, just as engineering tolerances do. Once one reaches the work standard, he goes no further. Once one is within the tolerances, he goes no further. The waste is obvious if you have read Chapter 4.

This point is one of the more difficult to understand. People think it very logical and orderly to work to a standard. They think that they need standards for material and financial planning. In fact, they do need figures for this planning, but they shouldn't get them from the "scientifically" fixed and politically negotiated work standards. They should, instead, listen to the process tell them what it is doing now, and then use these actual figures in their planning.

Many people who advocate systems that only pay for good parts produced and not on the sheer numbers demanded by the work standard, do not understand the difference between special and common causes of variation. This is true even though they advocate the supposedly reinforcing practice of "giving" pay instead of "taking away" pay. They miss the point. Did other inputs to the processing system contribute more to the "good" or "bad" outcomes than did the people? If so, you should not punish or reward the people as if they were the special cause for the particular outcome.

Work standards also tend to confuse the person's understanding of exactly what the job is. Are they to accomplish so many jobs per hour, or are they to meet the customer's needs? One such state of confusion existed in an office full of people charged with settling customers' claims. They also were evaluated on the number of calls they processed in a day and, in fact, had a work standard of 10 calls per hour. What was their job? You know exactly what it was. When a call approached six minutes in duration, they politely excused themselves and hung up, even though they hadn't met their customers' needs. Another case of your boss being your most important customer.

I think the key to understanding this point is found in the model of a process. The customer has a right to specify what he wishes. The process manager learns about those wishes through his customer feedback loop. Those wishes might be to have something in his hand on Thursday at 9 a.m., to have everyone reduce costs by 50% by January, or to have all white beads. However, before he takes action to meet those customers' needs, he must listen to his process through the process feedback loop.

A process manager gets into trouble whenever he listens exclusively either to the customer or the process. For instance, if he listens just to the process feedback loop, he runs the risk of losing the patient (customer) as Hans Bajaria portrayed at the 40th Annual ASQC meet in Anaheim, California.

If he listens to the customer feedback loop, he also runs the risk of losing the customer through increased costs. He does this by inappropriately reacting to the customer signal. He may follow three of the four rules of adjustment (Dr. Deming refers to them as the Nelson Funnel Experiment) and end up increasing variability and cost. Let me explain further what I mean by inappropriately reacting to the customer signal.

When a manager reacted only to the customer feedback loop, for instance, costs were reduced by only 35% by January. The resultant change that he makes in the incoming resources can be based on only one of two things:

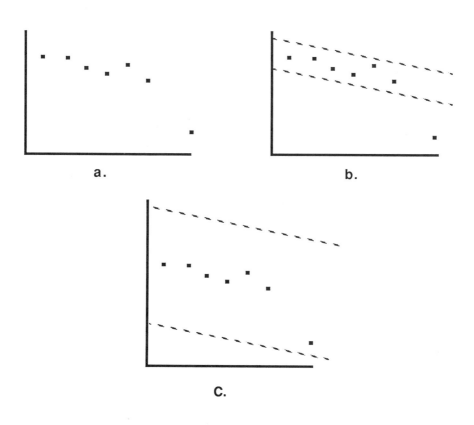

Figure 9-2

● Either the fact that only a 35% reduction was made was due to common cause variation that affected all process elements, in which case he might issue a letter to all employees to do or avoid doing a specific thing;

● Or he might react to those who did not make the 50% reduction and single them out for change.

Concentrating on the incoming resources is key to understanding why numerical goals and targets are inhibitors to continuing improvement. Any time you focus on the outcomes and not on the upstream process, you limit your ability to meet your customers' needs at a price they are willing to pay. The way the game has been played in the past is to give someone a figure or goal and they will back into it with a plan. The problem is compounded over the long term by a series of plans to reach short-term targets instead of one plan (with fine-tuning, of course) to reach a longer-term customer need. The longer-term plan should get you the intermediate results and put you in a better position to satisfy your customers' long-term needs because you are better able to recognize the need for system change.

In Figure 9-2a, we see the first six points as historical data. Management has determined that the seventh point will be the next period's target, a 50% reduction of cost. Now, management may be as arbitrary or as informed as they like; this is not the issue. This might seem like an ambitious goal, but you won't really know unless you analyze the data. They could show, as in Figure 9-2b, that the goal is outside the historical system and thus cannot be met unless the incoming resources of the process are reblended by management. The people who signed up for the goal, work in the system. Unless management changes the system, the people might do their best, but it will not be enough to meet the goal.

If the data from the process feedback loop show that the target is a part of the system, as in Figure 9-2c, then the people on the job at least have a chance to meet it.

Chapter 10

Institute leadership. The aim of leadership should be to help people, machines and gadgets to do a better job. Supervision of management is in need of overhaul, as well as supervision of production workers. (Point 7)

Dr. Deming changed the wording on the short form of this point. It used to read "Improve supervision." But the more he listened and observed and learned what was actually happening, the more he realized that supervision didn't exist. To improve something, it must already exist. Therefore, the job must be to institute it and then improve it. The change from supervision to leadership was suggested by James Fitzpatrick of General Motors. Bill Conway has observed for a number of years that more of a "follow me" mentality must exist in our managers instead of "I'm behind you all the way."

First line supervisors have perhaps the toughest job in any organization. They are people without a country. Their people do not consider them "one of the boys" and management does not really consider them part of the management team. The waste of this kind of arrangement accrues as the supervisor identifies with each group at his convenience. When he tells his people that management doesn't know what the hell they are doing, or when he tells management that his people just don't care, he contributes to the destruction of vital vertical teamwork.

A supervisor must be more than a judge or overseer as the name implies. In this new economic age, he must be a coach and a teacher. The prime responsibility of a supervisor must be to develop his people so that they continually improve, so they can do a better job. What does supervision do today? They do paperwork. As much as top management wishes for supervision to be people oriented, management systems force them to be paper oriented. What makes matters worse is what is on the paper. It is typically a count of outcomes that is used to feed other managers' hunger for the micromanagement of outcomes. Many people feel more comfortable managing things than people. They have never been trained to manage people. And even if they had been, all of the questions and the emphasis are on the outcomes which serve to reinforce that the important job is managing things and not people.

While we are talking about "things", however, Dr. Deming has observed that few supervisors or foremen have had the opportunity to participate in the processes that their people manage. If this is so, how can they be coaches who give advice or teach? The growth of specialization has seen to it that a supervisor need only send his people to the training department. The supervisor, of course, is proficient in filling out the training request form.

This new economic age presents challenges never before encountered by Western managers. This means that just "getting back to basics" will not be sufficient for success in the future.

If the challenge were simply more choices and a faster flow, we could meet it with more organization and more speed—that is, with traditional time management and strategic planning. But we are also dealing with a rogue element: new choices, possibilities that have not been seen and dealt with before. Preprogrammed solutions, habits, and previous personal experience may not work. Peak performers recognize that they are making not merely more choices, but new choices as well. The skills for handling "more and faster" do not always work with "new." . . . New requires learning, training, experimentation, and integration.[46]

New, as stated in Chapter 2, requires the need to understand some statistical thinking. And that requires some education and training.

Chapter 11

Institute training on the job. (Point 6)

Changing company systems alone will not assure continuing improvement. We must recognize a continuing training and education commitment to all employees. To put it in perspective, many of our Japanese competitors provide at least one year of training before they give anyone sole responsibility for a job. This training goes a long way towards ensuring that the employee fully understands his total job, the policies of the company, and his customers' and suppliers' needs. Genichi Taguchi told me several years ago that the Japanese plant manager faces much the same pressures to reduce cost that his American counterpart does. He has flexibility to cut costs in many areas, but one area he cannot reduce is his training budget, because training and education are the cornerstones of greater consistency.

If training is so important, why hasn't it been very effective? It hasn't been very effective because of a series of inhibitors. Because management has not changed company systems to use the training, untold millions of dollars are being wasted on training.

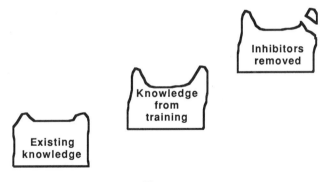

Figure 11-1

Training typically deepens the knowledge a person has about a subject. However, if you do not remove the barriers to using that knowledge, then it remains untapped.

The following scene is repeated the world over. An employee returns to work from a week or a day of training. His boss greets him with "A lot of work has piled up while you were gone, get to it. We have a schedule to meet and can't afford to slow down." We say essentially the same thing to our incoming college graduates, "We'll show you how it's done in the real world."

Several additional inhibitors to training are worth discussing here.

INHIBITORS TO TRAINING

It's for my people, not for me.

It's for manufacturing, not for me.

Our problems are different here.

We rely on our experience.

Hope for instant pudding

People learn in different ways.

Figure 11-2

It's for my people, not for me. Management is very busy. They feel that they do not have the time for the details of this kind of technical material. Yet it is they who need the details the most since most of the improvement is in their hands. They are directly competing with people who do understand statistical thinking. Management cannot intelligently change company systems without an understanding of statistical thinking.

If management realized how absolutely vital they are to their organization's understanding and use of statistical methods, they would not hesitate to participate. One method I have found effective is to have managers learn from their superiors and, in turn, train the people who report directly to them until all have been trained. Everyone in the organization except the top and the bottom person would go through the training twice, once as a subordinate and the next time as the supervisor. These kinds of actions speak volumes as to management's commitment. I first observed the benefits of this when Dr. Ed Baker and I visited Ford-do-Brazil to train their management in Dr. Deming's philosophy. I was worried that I did not speak Portuguese and thus could not train people very far down in the organization. (Only the top management throughout the Ford world needs to speak English.) I soon realized that this really was a blessing. Their people could not learn the system except through them, and the significance of that responsibility resulted in management learning and participating and teaching.

It's for manufacturing, not for me. Similar to the previous inhibitor which cut down through the organization, this one cuts across the organization. It is not hard to see why many nonmanufacturing people feel this way because of the paucity of nonmanufacturing examples and applications. If training is to be successful companywide, it must demonstrate a broad range of applications. The theory is universal, but you will be talking to the wall if people cannot see the theory applying to their jobs. There are numerous nonmanufacturing examples. Some critical characteristics are listed below.

Time to process a customer request
Errors in laboratory practices
Time for supplier to notify company of problem
Errors in filling dealer orders
Time to process travel expense reports
Time to process engineering changes
Number of word processing revisions
Wasted person-hours due to late starting meetings
Errors in accounts receivable
Size of accounting variances
Transit time of material
Number of engineering design changes

Figure 11-3

I am seeing more and more applications in nonmanufacturing areas. The following advertisement shows that quality can be a major force in the service industries.

QUALITY INC.

We spared no expense. The best Club of this type ever built anywhere in the USA. Sauna, Hot Tub, Waterbeds, Wide Screen TV, beautiful masseuses and NOW our new room.

THE SKYLIGHT ROOM

Also receive as a bonus, a free month membership with this coupon.

Figure 11-4

Our problems are different here. These methods and philosophies don't apply to us, we are a low volume producer, a job shop, primarily engineering. You must understand our business; have you ever worked in St. Louis?[32] I continue to frequently encounter all these statements and more. I respond to these challenges by saying that all processes are generically the same and that Dr. Deming's philosophy certainly applies to them. This answer, however, is quickly dismissed as rhetoric and I then usually must take the time to give them some gossip.

We rely on our experience. Experience teaches nothing. If experience taught us something, why are we in such a mess?[33]

Dr. Deming once asked Walter Shewhart what book influenced him the most. Shewhart's reply was *Mind and the World Order* by Clarence Irving Lewis. Dr. Deming then read the book and told Shewhart that it was very difficult to understand. Shewhart told him to start with Chapter 6. I would go even further toward the back of the book. I recommend that you read Chapters 10 and 11 first, but only after you have attended a Deming seminar. If you do read this book, you will find the source of enumerative and analytical thinking, experience teaches nothing, empirical knowledge is never complete, the need for operational definitions, and other nuances of the Deming philosophy. I do not want to intimidate you, but I quote from the book's back cover:

> Starting with the assumption that there are two systems of truth (abstract mathematical certainty, and secondly, empirical truth—or application of abstract truth to sense experiences), the author demonstrates that the traditional understanding of the *a priori* must be abandoned. Chapters discuss philosophy, metaphysics, philosophic method; the given element in experience; pure concepts; common concepts; knowledge of objects; relativity of knowledge; the a priori; the nature of the a priori;...This book is of interest not only to the specialist in philosophy, but also to the reader interested in the common ground where mathematics and philosophy meet. [34]

Most of the examples in Dr. Deming's book and in this one come from places where the people were relying on their experience to solve their problems. They did not have the statistical knowledge to recognize the problem/opportunity, much less the solution. The only reason the examples made it into these books is because someone was there who understood theory enough to ask the right questions. (More on this in Chapter 14.)

Hope for instant pudding. Dr. Deming first heard this expression from Jim Bakken, Vice President, Ford Motor Company. I think it very aptly describes many a manager's need for short-term results. "Just tell me the statistical formula and I will use it." The formulae have been around for years; there are no secrets. But there is no shortcut for understanding it and applying it. It takes time. Management are signing their people up for 3- to 5-day courses in statistical process control and expect them to change overnight. It cannot be done. As one buyer observed, "They trained us for 25 years to be attack dogs. Now after three days of training they want to give us to children as pets."

I see more and more advertisements touting SPC calculators or computer software that will solve your quality problems if you just install them. Instant experts offering just as quick solutions are popping up everywhere. Dr. Deming still gets calls from managers imploring him to "Come, spend a day with us and do for us what you did for Japan."

Another dimension to instant pudding is observed by Ralph H. Kilmann in his book "Beyond the Quick Fix".

> It is time to stop perpetuating the myth of simplicity. The system of organization invented by mankind generates complex problems that cannot be solved by simple solutions...Essentially, it is not the single approach of culture, strategy, or restructuring that is inherently ineffective. Rather, each is ineffective only if it is applied by itself—as a quick fix...The only alternative is to develop a truly integrated approach.[35]

Dr. Deming's contribution of over 35 years ago was to look at production as an integrated system, including all of the disciplines needed to run a business. Many had viewed quality and, in fact, other business processes as individual entities, not necessarily recognizing the synergistic effect on the whole. He said then, and he says now, that the change must be company-wide and nationwide. But it will not take place without some education. And as Professor Yoshida Tsuda told me, "You also need the wisdom to use the education."

Some Methods for Improvement

Statistical thinking will one day be as necessary for efficient citizenship as the ability to read and write. H. G. Wells

Part of creating the environment for continuing improvement is to provide all employees with a broad understanding of statistical thinking and statistical methods. These are powerful tools in helping identify action opportunities for continuing improvement. Management especially needs these tools to effectively manage their organizations. Bill Conway, former CEO of Nashua Corporation and now an internationally known management consultant, related this story to Ford management on the importance of the right tools:

> Let's suppose we are going to have a little contest. And so I take Bill and Charlie to my office and tell each of them that if he wins the contest he will have a big pension, take his family on an

around-the-world cruise, and otherwise be set for the rest of his life. Each of them is motivated and enthused about doing the job. They couldn't have better attitudes. I now explain that the contest consists of putting five wood screws into a pine board. I give each the screws and a board. But before the contest begins I give Charlie a little technical tool. I give him a screwdriver. Bill will just have to do the best he can. Well the contest begins and Charlie obviously wins and Bill is still saying that Charlie wasn't playing by the same rules. Of course he wasn't. He was using everything he had at his disposal. He would be dumb if he didn't.[36]

Statistical methods are not proprietary. They are available to anyone able to use them (and even to those not able to use them). In this new economic age, you would be dumb not to use them. No one method alone will suffice in your effort to understand what you are managing. Each tool has its strengths and weaknesses, and there is no substitute for knowledge in this area. I will discuss the following tools in this chapter:

Control charts
Flow diagrams
Cause and effect diagrams
Histograms
Pareto diagrams
Scatter diagrams
Check sheets
Other graphs
Design of experiments
Methods used by Taguchi

The above tools are obviously just a short listing of a much larger set of improvement methods. It is not my intention to present the details on these statistical and other improvement methods. Those may be found in various statistical books. Some of the books (in addition to Dr. Deming's) that I have found particularly useful include:

Continuing Process Control and Process Capability Improvement (Ford Motor Company, 1985)
Kaoru Ishikawa, *Guide to Quality Control* (UNIPUB, 1983)
Statistical Quality Control Handbook (Western Electric, 1954)
Transformation of American Industry Training System (QIP Inc., 1984)

But before you read any of these books, you must read and understand a paper by Dr. Deming titled "Boundaries of Statistical Inference". Much of the theory you have learned and will learn is useful for what Dr. Deming calls **enumerative** situations. Unfortunately, much of the real world management decisions focuses around **analytic** situations. As Dr. Deming has written:

"The aim of a statistical study is to provide a basis for action. In an enumerative study, action will be taken on material termed the universe, which is covered sufficiently well by the frame to be studied. Only substantive knowledge (engineering, psychology, medicine, agriculture, consumer research) can bridge the gap between the frame and the universe when they are not identical. In an analytic study, action will be taken on a cause-system or process with the hope of changing product of the future (which might be people, manufactured product, or agricultural product).

Briefly, an enumerative aim is to count or evaluate something. The uses to be made of an enumerative study depend only on the evaluation of a specified frame.

Some examples are the following:

1. An inventory of materials to assess their total value in dollars. This evaluation may determine the selling price, or evaluation for an auditor's report, or be for tax purposes.
2. Examination of equipment to estimate cost of maintenance.
3. The census of the U.S. for the purpose of Congressional representation.
4. Census of a city taken in an attempt to justify greater financial benefit from the state.
5. Evaluation of accounts receivable.

When there is an earthquake or a flood, a vital question is how many people, adults, infants, and infirm are there in need of the necessities of life. The aim is not to try to find out why so many people lived there, nor how to foretell the coming of an earthquake.

"In contrast, in an analytic study the aim is to seek causes. A firm advertises in order to change people, to change their tastes and habits. The firm conducts consumer research to learn how effective a scheme of promotion was last month, the aim being to acquire ideas on how to advertise more effectively in the future. Why do people buy this brand and not some other? A study of accounts receivable, primarily for an enumerative purpose, may also yield information by which errors can be reduced in the future. Why are there so many errors of this or that type in the accounts receivable? What are some of the special causes of variation of a particular dimension? What are some of the common causes?

"We may generalize to say that in an enumerative study, the aim is to evaluate some numerical characteristic of a frame, not to study the causes that made the frame what it is. The action to be taken will be disposition of the frame. In contrast, in an analytic study, the aim is to discover causes to find out what made the frame what it is, and how to modify the process that will produce frames that we desire to see in the future.

"One can only learn theory. One can only teach theory. The question is what theory? What modifications of theory now in the books and in the classroom are desirable in the teaching of the design of experiments and surveys?

"First, let me mention the testing of hypotheses. This is beautiful theory, with errors of the first and second kind, and power of a test. What the books fail to point out is that this theory applies only to enumerative studies. No such beauty of theory exists in an analytic study. People certainly make errors of the second kind and other wrong decisions in business, law, agriculture, medicine, and manufacturing processes. However, that it is rarely possible to evaluate from comparisons of Method A and Method B the probability of being wrong in actually adopting Method A over Method B. One may state categorically without spending a nickel that $\mu a \neq \mu b$. We don't need an experiment for that. The statistical question to be answered is what is the magnitude of μa-μb under specified ranges of conditions, and does the difference warrant the expense of a change? What is the cost of change? How sure are we that the difference is big enough to warrant this expense? The problem is estimation and economics, not a matter of testing a hypothesis. Only substantive knowledge can bridge the gap between (a) the frame and conditions studied and (b) the cause-system that will produce other frames under other conditions. A doctor of medicine or a chemist may, over his own signature, assert by substantive knowledge that a test carried out on patients in Chicago would give the same results in Denver. No statistical theory can make such a generalization. Statistical theory ends with inference about the frame and the conditions studied.[37]

The point is, many a decision is legitimized by the misapplication of statistical inference in an analytical situation, where you do not have a frame. It is not that you cannot do the calculations, it is just that they do not mean anything in regard to the future. In making any decision you must balance your knowledge of the subject matter with your knowledge from statistics. It is rarely either/or.

Graduates in mathematical statistics, when taking up practice, discover yawning gaps between theory and practice; the better their theoretical training, the wider the gap.[38]

If we look back at the process model, we can see that in a process used for the detection of defects (remember a pure feed-forward system), the use of statistical methods is primarily for enumerative purposes. That is, you are only concerned about understanding, making inferences about, and taking action on the outcomes (read frame) that you have before you. Any link with other frames is only accomplished by your knowledge of other subject matter and not by statistical theory.

THE PROCESS USED FOR THE DETECTION OF DEFECTS

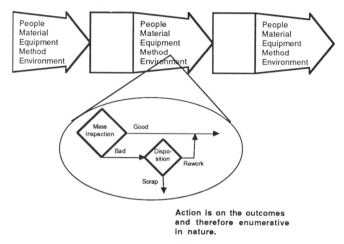

Action is on the outcomes
and therefore enumerative
in nature.

Figure 11-5

In a process used for the prevention of defects (remember a pure feedback system), the use of statistical methods is primarily for analytic purposes. That is, you are concerned about taking action on the cause system that produced the outcomes. This action will affect future outcomes, not the existing ones. There is no frame from which to make inferences about, using statistical theory.

THE PROCESS USED FOR THE PREVENTION OF
DEFECTS

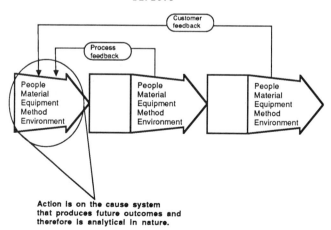

Action is on the cause system
that produces future outcomes and
therefore is analytical in nature.

Figure 11-6

With that as background, I will briefly discuss some of the uses of a few of the improvement tools.

Control Charts. A control chart is the one statistical tool that enables many of the other statistical tools to be used in this world, not just the theoretical one. This is because it gives evidence on the lack of applicability of certain theoretical assumptions used by the other tools, assumptions such as randomness, equal variances, independence of outcomes, and the like.

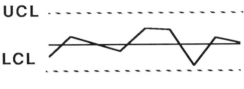

Figure 11-7

Dr. Walter Shewhart of the Bell Laboratories first made the distinction between controlled and uncontrolled variation due to what we call common and special causes while studying process data in the 1920's. He developed a simple but powerful tool to dynamically separate the two—the control chart. Since that time, control charts have been used successfully in a wide variety of process control situations, both in the U.S. and other countries, notably Japan. Experience has shown that control charts effectively direct attention toward special causes of variation when they appear and reflect the extent of common cause variation that must be reduced by management action.

Several types of control charts have been developed to analyze both variables and attributes. However, all control charts have the same two basic uses. Using Shewhart's terms, they are:

● As a judgement, to give evidence whether a process has been operating in a state of statistical control, and to signal the presence of special causes of variation so that corrective action can be taken.

● As an operation, to maintain the state of statistical control, by extending the control limits as a basis for real-time decisions.[15]

Special Causes of variation can be detected by simple statistical techniques. These causes of variation are not common to all the operations involved. The discovery of a special cause of variation, and its removal, are usually the responsibility of someone who is directly connected with the process, although management sometimes is in a better position to correct.

The extent of **common causes** of variation can be indicated by simple statistical techniques, but the causes themselves need more detailed analysis to isolate. These common causes of variation are usually the responsibility of management to correct, although other people directly connected with the process sometimes are in a better position to identify these causes and pass them on to management for correction.

People many times equate the statement that 85% of the opportunities for improvement are management's responsibility, with the definition of common causes of variation. Likewise, 15% of the opportunities are the worker's responsibility and are special causes of variation. This is a common misunderstanding. The implication is that 85% of the time the process is in control and it is management's responsibility to improve upon it, and 15% of the time special causes are evident and the worker is responsible for correcting them. In reality, special causes of variation can be persuaded to "pop out" depending on your sampling plan. Even so, a change of material may be detected on the control chart as a special cause, but the local operator does not buy the stuff—purchasing does. An individual might consistently overestimate costs on his expense report. He will probably be in control at the level and yet he has direct control of the needed change.

One bad byproduct of the 85/15, common/special cause misunderstanding is a sense of feeling unimportant by the local worker because he can only affect 15% of the problems or opportunities. Why bother? This can be devastating, since an organization needs everyone contributing to improvement. It is for this reason that I added the last sentence to the common cause definition. Management may be the only ones who can really do something about the opportunity for improvement, but they cannot act if they do not know about it. Many times the local process manager is the one who observes the opportunity. And unless he alerts management so that they may act, nothing will happen. So the individual process managers are indeed very important. They not only greatly affect about 15% of the opportunities for improvement, but also affect the 85% of the opportunities which are someone else's responsibility.

A control chart is an economic tool. It balances the economics of looking for special causes when none exist, and not looking when they do exist. It lets the process talk to you. Control limits are *not* specification limits. They only depend on what the process is actually doing and, of course, the way you choose to sample from it.

Management is paid to make decisions which affect the future. They have a better chance of actually affecting the future as they think they will if they are making a decision on a process in statistical control. You notice that I did not say that the decision would be right or wrong, or better or worse; that is dependent on your knowledge of the particular subject matter. We saw in Chapter 3 that there is a distribution of outcomes in any process. A process in statistical control will have essentially the same shape, location, and spread over time.

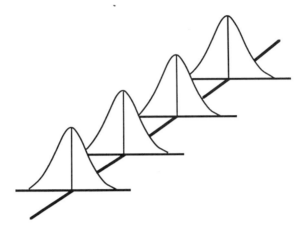

Figure 11-8

A manager making a decision based on the first set of data should affect the future as he planned because the conditions on which he based the decision are holding through time. But in the real world, stability, or the existence of a system, is seldom a natural state. It is an achievement, the result of eliminating special causes one by one on statistical signal, leaving only the random variation of a stable process.[2]

A process might change from time to time because of a shifting average.

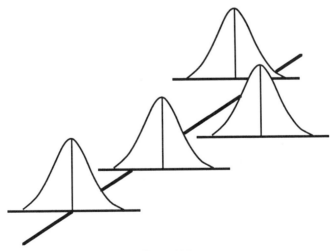

Figure 11-9

It also might change because of shifting variability.

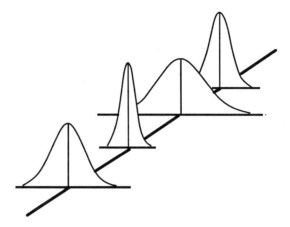

Figure 11-10

And, as we all know, in the real world we see a combination of shifting means and variances as well as shapes.

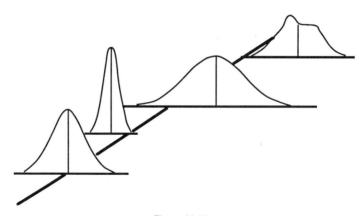

Figure 11-11

You never really see these pictures, but a control chart can signal you when there are changes in the mean and variance.

There is no substitute for managing your own process with these tools to gain a better understanding of their power. These following statements should make better sense after you have had a chance to study about and then use control charts. Some of the shortcomings and false starts I have observed include (they are in no special order):

● Charting a characteristic at a stage in the process where you couldn't readily take action on a special cause. I typically see charts too far downstream in a process to do any real good because the cause of an out-of-court signal could be any of a million possibilities.

● Not reacting to signals of special causes because of production pressures. Someone once remarked to me that I really didn't think that he could stop the production line just to find the source of an out-of-control signal, did I?

● Not reacting to signals of special causes because they were nowhere near making any out-of-specification parts.

● Not reacting to signals of special causes because there is no action plan to guide the process manager.

● Not reacting to signals of special causes because control limits are not based on the data. Instead, they are based on a percentage of the specifications or some other arbitrary line based on experience. The result is either overcontrol or undercontrol.

● Not reacting to signals of special causes because the control limits have not been recalculated when they should have been.

● Not reacting to signals of special causes (specifically runs above or below the center line) because there is no center line plotted.

● Inappropriate sampling scheme, usually five pieces taken randomly throughout the shift.

● Management punishes bad news, so people do anything to keep the process in control. Things such as sampling until a "good" part comes along, keeping the charts neat, sampling five per shift, and using modified control limits are often used to keep management happy. Those tactics also keep you in the dark.

● Total dependence on an SPC facilitator when quality is a line responsibility. It is very easy and convenient to rely on a facilitator. This is short-term thinking and a difficult loop to get out of. Be careful how you make the transition, however. I have seen a plant use the facilitator for charting while giving the operator discretion to screen out "bad" parts before they are used. Obviously, the control charts done by the facilitator are of limited value because some bad parts never have a chance to be recorded.

● Lack of traceability on data or events which might lead to understanding causes for out-of-control signals. Often charts are "gundecked" after the fact and real time observations are not logged on the chart. Pressure for production paperwork places a premium on people who can print and not necessarily produce. Many supervisors treasure an employee who likes to do paperwork so the rest can get the work out and not be bothered with it.

Flow Diagrams can lead to understanding and improvement of the process. It can be as detailed or as general as you want.

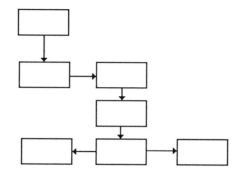

Figure 11-12

● Use teams of people to agree on the process flow. Even though there are very competent people, no one person has the perspective of the team. Time and time again I see the benefits of using a team. The teams should consist of your customer, your suppliers, an expert in the subject matter, and others that will help you meet your customers' needs.

● Many times, the process can easily be simplified or improved just by looking at the now-visible process flow. Before it was put down on paper, the changes were not as obvious.

● Use a hierarchical approach. Start with your customer's most critical characteristic and work backward, going into as much detail as you need to understand what is happening.

Cause and Effect Diagrams are extremely important because they force people to think explicitly about the specifics of their process as well as their suppliers and customers. Once this is done, problem solving and improvement is greatly facilitated.

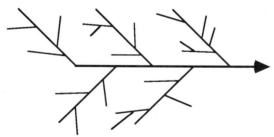

Figure 11-13

Management and others whose work is more art than science often say that they don't need to use a cause and effect diagram, that it is a waste of time as they use their experience in their jobs. But when we force the issue and sit down with them to construct one, they usually say that it was worthwhile because they hadn't thought of this or that specific source of variation. They also readily recognize the meaning of the phrase "Pay me now, or pay me later." Downtime costs a lot of money, and a large part of downtime can be troubleshooting time. Construction of cause and effect diagrams in advance can save a lot of trouble-shooting time.

There are a number of other benefits in using a cause and effect diagram:

• It is a tool that helps a team of people work together toward a common end. An individual cannot produce a cause and effect diagram that is as effective as is possible with a group. Brainstorming and other creative techniques are often used to construct the diagram.

• It is a valuable tool to build a list of potential causes of a quality problem or opportunity for improvement.

• It focuses on the cause of variability. Getting people to think about and identify causes of variability is a valuable education and will help future performance.

Histograms are perhaps one of the most misused statistical tools. They are effective only for data that come from a process that is in a state of statistical control. This is obviously the case in assessment of the capability of a process. The histogram can then give valuable graphic information on the distribution of individual outcomes.

Figure 11-14

If you make a decision based on the histogram shown, you might be making a big mistake. By turning the histogram on its side and showing the data in the order taken, we can see that there is an obvious trend taking place. Chances are, if the next point were taken it would follow the same

TIME ———▶

Figure 11-15

trend. This is something that you would not detect by just looking at the histogram.

There might be a run of seven or more above or below the center line to indicate existence of a special cause. Again, you would be making a big mistake if you only looked at the histogram.

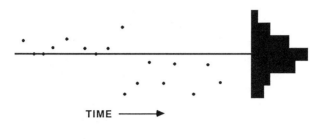

TIME ⟶

Figure 11-16

There are numerous examples of the pitfalls of looking only at a histogram or any other statistic which throws away the information that is contained in the order of generation of the data.

Ford Motor Company tests new robot models at their Robotics and Automation Applications Consulting Center. They subject some of the robots to a series of 17 tests to assess their performance for suitability to general process applications. The tests are conducted by exercise of the robot through a standardized series of moves at conditions of no-load and full-load after a one-half hour warm-up period. Measurements are made by a computerized system of noncontact gauges. In one test, the arm is swept horizontally through a 135 degree arc.

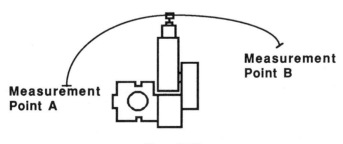

Measurement Point B

Measurement Point A

Figure 11-17

A histogram of 1,000 readings from point A appears to be reasonable enough. It is centered on 0 and ranges from plus or minus 6 thousandths of an inch.

Figure 11-18

However, the data (shown in order of appearance) show a definite downward trend. The manufacturer had recommended a warm-up period of one half hour. The test showed that the machine had still not settled down, even after one and a half hours. Would calculations of the average and standard deviation mean anything if you needed to make a decision on the future use of the robot? No.

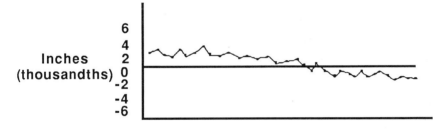

Figure 11-19

A very useful derivative of a histogram was created by John Tukey[39]. It is called the Stem and Leaf Plot. It shows the central tendency and spread as well as the shape (dependent on the number of stems, of course). It additionally preserves the actual recorded numerical values.

Stem	Leaves
0	4 1 3
0	9 7 6 8
1	3 0 3 4 2 0 0 4 3 2 1
1	5 9 5 7 7
2	3 2
2	6

Figure 11-20

Remember to always plot the data in order of time. There is nothing unusual in this plot of the data, so perhaps the shape and central tendency and dispersion will be of some value to you.

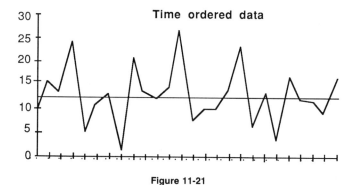

Figure 11-21

Pareto Diagrams (more correctly known as Juran Diagrams) are another basic graphic aid useful for focus on the solution of problems or action on opportunities for improvement.

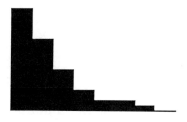

Figure 11-22

The primary use of Pareto diagrams is to focus efforts on improvement on the most important causes. It is common for about 80% of the problems to result from only about 20% of the potential causes. This is very fortunate, because we have only a limited number of resources to expend at any one time.

You must be careful, however, not to use blindly a Pareto diagram assuming that it is log-normally distributed and that the top few causes are any different from the others. As I pointed out in Chapter 5, the question is not who or what is ranked number one or last, the question is who or what is inside or outside the system. Once management is aware of the answer, improvement may be pursued.

J.D. Power & Associates publish a Customer Satisfaction Index derived from their annual survey of automotive customers. In 1983 the rankings were as follows:

Rank	Score	Carline
1	159	Mercedes-Benz
2	137	Toyota
3	135	Subaru
4	124	Honda
5	118	Mazda
6	115	Volvo
7	114	Lincoln-Mercury
8	110	BMW
9	108	Saab
9	108	Porsche-Audi
11	107	Ford
12	103	Mitsubishi
13	101	Jaguar
13	101	Nissan
15	98	Volkswagen
16	93	Dodge
17	92	Oldsmobile
18	90	Chrysler-Plymouth
19	83	Chevrolet
20	81	Isuzu
20	81	Cadillac
22	80	Buick
23	77	Pontiac
24	76	American Motors
25	60	Renault

Figure 11-23

This rank order by score implies that there is a difference between carlines. Let's look at the data in Pareto diagram form.

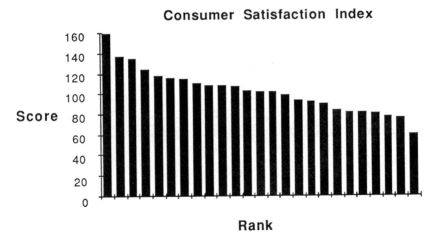

Consumer Satisfaction Index

Figure 11-24

Are they all part of the same system? Some simple calculations will show that the average score is about 102 and an estimate of the standard deviation of the data is about 22. A system is defined as data between the average plus and minus 3 standard deviations. That is, $102 + 66 = 168$ and $102 - 66 = 46$ define the system limits. You can see that none of the data fall outside these limits. Therefore, you really cannot distinguish between the data. However, if for seven years in a row, a carline was always in a particular position or was continually increasing or decreasing, then there would be a basis to rule this carline out of the system—not part of the system.

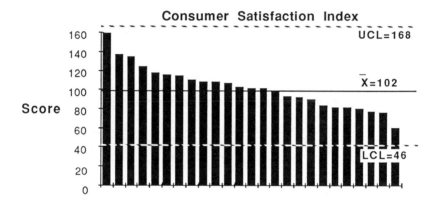

Figure 11-25

Scatter Diagrams are extremely useful for examination of possible relationships between data. This relationship, however has nothing to do with cause and effect.

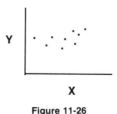

Figure 11-26

For instance, Gross National Product might correlate well with the amount of time wasted waiting for meetings to start. But it would be ludicrous to think that wasting more time waiting for meetings to start would raise the GNP.

I have seen people dutifully draw a straight line through the strangest pattern of points. So don't needlessly assume linearity. The most important thing that you can do is to look at the data. Don't be impressed with a sight unseen correlation coefficient (r) or coefficient of determination (r²). To help calibrate your eyeball, I have included the following plots from a soon-to-be-published book by Victor Kane entitled *Defect Prevention: Use of Simple Statistical Tools* (Marcel Dekker, Inc.).

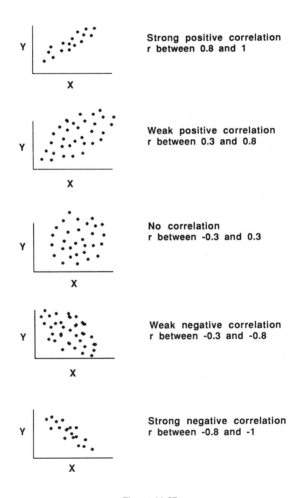

Figure 11-27

Many books will mention that X is a predictor of Y (or vice versa). You must be careful to note that you cannot put any number on that predictability.

The correlation holds for past data and not necessarily future data. As you saw earlier in this chapter, only your knowledge of the subject matter can help you for analytical purposes.

The basic purpose of a **Check Sheet** is to make collection of information easy and to provide data that will be accumulated for possible later analysis.

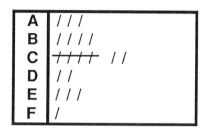

Figure 11-28

The following benefits of using check sheets comes from a Ford Motor Company course entitled "A System to Establish Defect Prevention and Use of Problem Identification Tools":

• Many measurements are currently being made for the purpose of producing parts within the specification limits. Check sheets provide a tool for quick record and later analysis of the process.

• A usable historical record of the process performance is available from past check sheets.

• Use of check sheets provides a possible tool of transition to go from no collection of data to effective use of other statistical methods.

You should note that merely recording problems will not lead to any permanent resolution of the problem. It is extremely important to identify the root causes of a problem and eliminate the causes. Individuals at all levels must be prepared to act both to find a root cause and to take steps to eliminate the cause. Failure to act in either case says to employees that no one cares about problems or opportunities for improvement.

Graphs can greatly improve management's productivity. Instead of poring through reams of tables and numbers, management can see quickly the

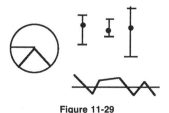

Figure 11-29

trends or other information with graphs. Even if they insist on the implied preciseness of tables and numbers, they also may use the graphs.

I have mentioned earlier that management is paid to make decisions that affect the future. Dr. Deming has often said that in business you get beat up a lot or a little depending on your mistakes. In order to make decisions, management needs information. There are many vehicles for this information, but the one I will now discuss is **management reports,** and specifically, ones which contain numerical data. Before you read any further, answer this question:

Why do you want the report?
a. Because your boss gets it.
b. You just want to know what's happening.
c. Because this position has always gotten it.
d. You need to make a decision.
e. You want to audit your organization.
f. It will help your performance review.
g. _____.

Figure 11-30

Obviously, some answers are better than others, but management has commissioned and maintained reports for all of the above reasons and more, most of which result in the waste of time. However, if you determine that you absolutely, positively must have the report, then try to use the following guidelines:

• Use control charts. Your decisions affect the future and can be more effective if you know that the basis for your decision is predictable and is in control. This information also directs the type of decision because of your recognition of common causes or special causes and the appropriate action for each.

• Use graphics wherever possible. If you insist on the implied preciseness of tables of numbers, use graphs also; they will increase your productivity. The illustrated summary report to management consisted of pages of numbers. Management could only react to numbers that they felt, based on their experience, were worthy of question.

MANAGEMENT SUMMARY REPORT			
	Current Performance	Previous Performance	MTD
Plant #1	(Insp/Rej.)	(Insp/Rej.)	(Insp/Rej.)
Road test	20/2	21/3	62/9
Final line	13371/1915	14769/2651	46407/7643
Final test	15500/1330	15637/1211	50173/3923
Main control	15092/1526	16452/1567	49808/4270
Water test	14227/787	14759/980	47230/3401
Plant #2			
Road test	11/0	1/0	
Final line	9178/315		
Final test	8382/5??		

Figure 11-31

The format was modified to include a graphic representation of the current performance to historical control limits. Management can now take advantage of statistical thinking in their decisions. By the way, what should they be concerned about in the report here?

MANAGEMENT SUMMARY REPORT		
	Current Performance	
Plant #1	(Insp/Rej.)	75 80 85 90 95 100
Road test	20/2	(------------------*----------------)
Final line	13371/1915	(--------*-------)
Final test	15500/1330	(--*--)
Main control	15092/1526	* (------)
Water test	14227/787	* (---)
Plant #2		
Road test	11/0	
Final line	9178/315	
Final test	8382/5??	

Figure 11-32

If you do not understand your responsibilities in this new economic age, you might suggest looking at the out-of-control signals in the current main control and water test processes. The latest results indicate that there is a special cause on the bad side. If you do understand management's responsibilities, you would notice that the control limits of the final line test are far wider than the other processes with equivalent sample sizes and will continue that way until management changes the process. (The road test control limits are wider because of the small sample size.) This is the important responsibility. Your people can correct the special causes. Only you can change the process in which your people operate.

● Show the information over time. Trends are extremely important information. There is enough short-term pressure without emphasizing it in a report.

● Use a range of estimates. The world is not deterministic. Numbers vary. Point estimates can be very misleading.

● Resist the temptation to aggregate and summarize too much. You lose sensitivity when you summarize. Rating systems often fall into this trap.

● Give your subordinates a longer wheelbase to recover. If you use the report for auditing your organization, and your subordinates use the same report daily to manage their part, you should get the report less often than daily.

Design of Experiments is a vital tool in continuing improvement. Once a process is in control, the real improvement can begin. It can begin because of our ability to plan (Deming Cycle Step 1) and then analyze (Deming Cycle Step 3) more than one variable at a time. We continuously experiment as we manage our processes. There is nothing mysterious about experimenting. However, many can play catch, but only a few can juggle.

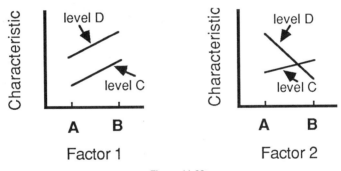

Figure 11-33

For less complex problems in days gone by, the experimentation process was relatively straightforward (like playing catch), albeit sometimes lengthy. A "scientific" approach to experimentation was to vary one factor while holding other factors constant. When, after a series of runs, the outcomes reached certain criteria, the tests were concluded and action was taken. Even today, many people use this approach to experimentation. If you had nine factors (which is not at all unusual) you needed to vary at only two levels each, you would need to make 512 experimental runs.

Today's complex problems will require more time (and money) if the one-at-a-time test approach is used. Additionally, we now recognize that there may be complex interactions between factors whose effects cannot be measured by the one-at-a-time approach. A well-planned experiment could reduce the need for 512 runs to 32 and, in addition, begin to get information on factor interactions. Time and money are saved and valuable information is gained for improvement purposes.

Unfortunately, because of short-term performance pressures, today's manager might only have enough in his budget for one or two runs. The issue from management's perspective is not a dramatic four-fold decrease in the number of runs required (from 512 to 32). It is a 32-fold increase (from 1 to 32)!

A technology in the research and development (R&D) stage has just completed a standard 1,000-hour test. Based on the successful test, it leaves the R&D stage, with few or no problems. The only real problem was the R&D program itself. Why was the test duration 1,000 hours? Why not 100 hours? Why not 100,000 hours? In this case, if the test were less than the 1,000 hours, the R&D cost would have been reduced and the technology could have been on the street sooner. Instead, the 1,000 hours of testing was chosen because it was "standard;" everyone tested them for 1,000 hours.

If engineers understood some statistical theory, their experiment might be better planned and their results more useful to the overall organization's mission. I need to caution the casual user of the traditional experimental analysis technique of Analysis of Variance (ANOVA). This is a very powerful enumerative tool. But it is incorrectly used many times in analytic situations. Ron Moen, Lloyd Provost, and Tom Nolan, who are statistical consultants, are refining experimental techniques for use in analytical situations.

Methods Used by Taguchi

There is considerable interest nowadays among people in management to train everyone in "Taguchi Methods." They perceive these methods to be newer and thus superior to those that Dr. Deming has been trying to get us to use to manage our businesses. I think this is a mistake. First of all, they are not new. The statistical methods he advocates have been around for decades and are a subset of experiment design techniques discussed above. And second, they are not superior or necessarily easier to understand and use. In fact, no single statistical tool has ever been universally superior. Each has its place in a manager's tool box. Now, there is much that I do not understand about Taguchi's approach to quality. But nevertheless, I want to highlight where I think his approach could be used as an integral part of Dr. Deming's philosophies. I will also comment on areas that I perceive as incompatible.

Right away we see an apparent conflict. Taguchi defines quality as "The loss imparted to the society from the time a product is shipped." The key word in the definition is "loss." It gives a negative connotation to something that Dr. Deming views as very positive. He defines quality as "Continually meeting customers' needs and expectations at a price that they are willing to pay." In order to reconcile this difference (and we can), we must understand Taguchi's view of loss.

First of all, he recognizes that there is an incremental economic loss for any deviation from a customer specified target. This view is quite different from the traditional view that there is no loss so long as the parts are within the engineering tolerances. Dr. Taguchi's view has its roots in some of Dr. Deming's earlier teachings.

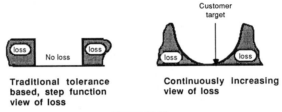

Traditional tolerance based, step function view of loss

Continuously increasing view of loss

Figure 11-34

Taguchi defines loss as being caused by functional variation of the product which he calls "noise." There are three types of noise:

- Outer noise, which is the variation of environmental conditions such as temperature, humidity, customer usage, etc.
- Inner noise, which is the deterioration of elements or materials.
- Variational noise, which is the piece-to-piece variability of products.

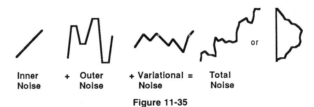

Figure 11-35

This is just another way of categorizing the sources of variation. And in fact, these noises take the familiar form of people, materials, methods, equipment, and environment.

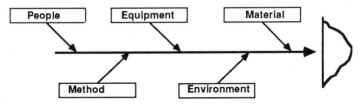

Figure 11-36

In order to minimize the loss caused by these noise sources, countermeasures are used. They include:

- Off-line countermeasures, and
- On-line countermeasures

He considers the off-line countermeasure of design as the more important of the two, which agrees with Dr. Deming's views to work upstream in design if you are to really reduce variation. There are three steps in the off-line countermeasure of design:

- **System Design**—The full use of specialized know-how, or as Dr. Deming says, knowledge of a substantive expert, is the focus of this step. We do a considerable amount of system design and, according to Taguchi, are very good at the innovation required in this step. We have a NASA mentality on quality, however, which says higher quality costs more. What actually makes it cost more is our uncertainty of what the customer really wants. Overdesign and its associated cost is the result of this uncertainty.
- **Parameter Design**—This step can result in higher quality at lower cost. This is accomplished by taking advantage of any nonlinear relationships between inputs and outcomes. Thus we can greatly reduce variability (noise) and achieve higher stability and a significant improvement of quality by using low cost inputs. Statistical methods, especially designed experiments, can be extremely helpful in this step. Taguchi advocates the use of orthogonal arrays, but other methods may be used as well. Taguchi feels that we typically skip this step and proceed directly to tolerance design from system design.
- **Tolerance Design**—This step, as in system design, results in higher quality but at a higher price. Again, here is a NASA mentality which calls for tightened tolerances to ensure consistency. This focus on the outcomes of a process and not the process itself results in higher costs.

To help your understanding of the interrelationships between the noises and their countermeasures, I will discuss each of the noises and how they can be reduced by the countermeasures.

Inner noise is the variability due to deterioration within a piece. For example: the resistance of a resistor increases by 10% in five years, plastic gets more brittle with age, a shaft wears with use, people get tired, policies get outdated or overtaken by events. If we look at the total variability of

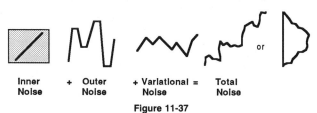

| Inner Noise | + | Outer Noise | + Variational Noise | = | Total Noise |

Figure 11-37

outcomes over time, inner noise can be the main contributor to the slope of the outcomes.

System Design can reduce inner noise, but only with the expenditure of more money. An engineer can incorporate redundancy, such as dual braking, with its added cost to mitigate deterioration. He can also specify screening or burn-in to eliminate those with high initial failures.

Parameter Design also reduces inner noise, but typically for a lot less money. This type of design looks to use nonlinearity where it is advantageous (cost effective) to do so.

Tolerance Design reduces inner noise, but, like system design, it, too, costs money. An engineer might choose to reduce wear by specifying a harder material or by going to precision tolerances.

On-Line Control methods have little or no effect on inner noise. They are too late.

Outer noise is the variation from the environment acting on the use of the product. For example: customers drive differently, divisions interpret policy and procedures differently, the greenbelt region is more corrosive than other regions, people understand Taguchi differently, etc. If we look at the total variability of outcomes over their life-cycle, outer noise can be a major contributor to wide swings in the outcomes.

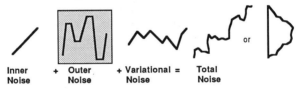

| Inner Noise | + | Outer Noise | + | Variational Noise | = | Total Noise |

Figure 11-38

System Design can reduce outer noise, but only with the expenditure of more money. An engineer might specify an automatic control system such as the EEC-IV (Electronic Engine Control—fourth generation) to minimize output variations by compensating for environmental changes such as temperature, humidity, barometric pressure, etc. An analyst might spend more time designing and testing a form which can be easily used by the entire organization.

Parameter Design also reduces outer noise, but typically for a lot less money. This type of design looks to use nonlinearity where it is advantageous (cost effective) to do so. For instance, the speed of the car has a nonlinear effect on the steering wheel vibration frequency at a given steering wheel spoke position. Additionally, a customer's sensitivity to vibration is lessened if the wheel has a higher harmonic vibration. A set of designed experiments identified this relationship and parameter design was used to locate the spoke to minimize the frequency variation over a wide range of vehicle speeds.

**Response curve for optimal
spoke position**

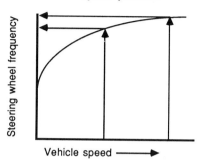

Figure 11-39

Tolerance Design has little or no effect on outer noise.

On-Line Control methods have little or no effect on outer noise. They are too late.

Variational Noise is the variability due to piece-to-piece differences in the production of outcomes. For example: camshaft weights are different, students' learning in a classroom setting is different, travel expense reports are different, etc.

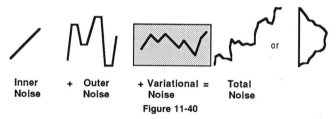

| Inner | + | Outer | + | Variational | = | Total |
| Noise | | Noise | | Noise | | Noise |

Figure 11-40

System Design can reduce variational noise, but only with the expenditure of more money. An engineer might design a process that momentarily stops to cut a piece of stock, thus giving more piece-to-piece consistency than a process which does not stop but gives more production. An engineer can spend even more money by designing a process that has a flying shear. The choice involves a tradeoff between variation and cost.

Parameter Design also reduces variational noise, but typically for a lot less money. This type of design looks to use nonlinearity where it is advantageous (cost effective) to do so.

Tolerance Design reduces variational noise but, like system design, it, too, costs money.

On-Line Control methods are especially suited to reduce variational noise.

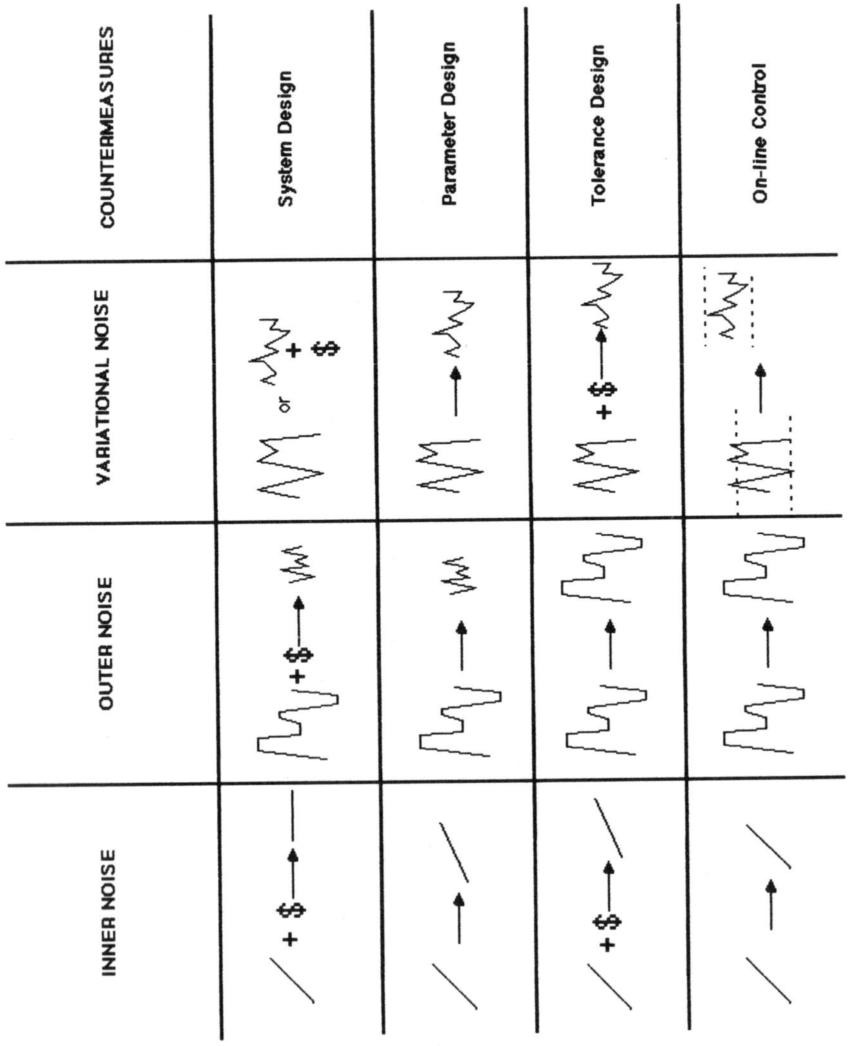

Figure 11-41

I think that Taguchi's view of on-line control methods presupposes that there already is good piece-to-piece consistency and statistical control. If this is not his view, then there may be problems reconciling his proposed methods with Shewhart's and others'.

The chart (Figure 11-41) summarizes the relationship between the noises which categorize variation and their countermeasures which reduce it in the customer's use. You will notice that not all countermeasures are useful against all noises. Also, as Dr. Deming says, you need to work upstream in the design to be truly effective in reducing variability, and this is precisely what Dr. Taguchi is advocating.

As I stated previously, there is much that I do not know about Taguchi's approach. From what I do understand, I think that many of the methods he is advocating have their place in your efforts to continually improve. If you wish to learn more, read his works.[40]

If you wish to learn more about blending Taguchi's approach with the Box, Hunter, and Hunter approach, contact the University of Wisconsin's Center for Quality and Productivity Improvement, 610 Walnut Street, Madison, WI 53705; or the American Supplier Institute, Six Parklane Boulevard, Suite 411, Dearborn, Michigan 48126.

Chapter 12

Institute a vigorous program of education and self-improvement. (Point 13)

As Dr. Deming's philosophy is instituted and organizations begin on the road to continuing improvement, there will be a reduced need for all incoming resources because of a reduction in waste. We will need less space, material, cumbersome and redundant methods, equipment, and people. As we reinvest in our other resources, we must reinvest in our most important asset, our people. Management must make it perfectly clear in the beginning that they will reinvest in their people. If they cannot make the commitment to lifetime employment, they must commit to using attrition for reduced people requirements. They will not get the necessary cooperation unless they make it clear that their people will not be working themselves out of a job. They may be working themselves out of an assignment, but not employment.

One well-respected company outsources at least 30 percent of major items in a plant, even though they have the capacity to produce them. This serves as a buffer for their employees against the cyclical vagaries of the business. The unfortunate thing is that the supplier is then faced with the layoffs because he is desourced as the business is brought back in house. The customer ends up paying for this suboptimization. It is the same thing as shifting your inventory to your supplier just so you can say that you have reduced your inventory. The costs are still in the system. It would be better for the whole system if we staffed for low periods and used overtime for peak periods. (But even this is not without its problems.) If you are not there yet, use attrition to get there.

In many instances, especially in good times, loss of employment is not a concern. There is a similar problem, however, and that is loss of overtime. Since management has been burned by overstaffing in the past, they prefer to use overtime instead of new hires to handle increased production require-ments. Some people get accustomed to the overtime, and if they improved productivity, would lose it. Management must be aware of these inhibitors and change the system to encourage the continuing improvement. Where people want the overtime, I have seen management train them in more than one job so that when they improve themselves out of overtime in one assignment, they may work it in another. This is a feasible short-term fix, but obviously this just postpones the inevitable as the need for overtime diminishes.

Management will recognize the need for education and retraining when they realize that people are an asset and not an expense. Dr. Deming has observed that management treats people as a commodity.

I met not long ago with forty skilled tradesmen. They were working overtime—sometimes two hours, sometimes three hours, but not knowing until Thursday of any week if they would be called back to the company the next week. They might be called and they might not. And one of them remarked, "We are a commodity." I saw the connection. They are a commodity on the commodities exchange. You don't have to buy anything today. You can defer it until tomorrow. You don't have to buy anything. They are commodities. They may be bought next week or they may not be. Naturally they ask for the highest price. If you had something for sale on the commodities exchange, I think you would be a fool to take anything but the highest price you could get for it. They are treated like a commodity—bought and sold like a commodity. People ask for security. People would like to know if they are going to have a job next week. And it's true with management as well, perhaps even more so. How can somebody devote his knowledge to the company and do it with devotion when he's not sure he will be there next week or next year? He'd be looking around for another job if he had any sense or ability.[41]

In one of my trips to Japan, I learned how several Deming Medal companies invest in their people through the commitment of lifetime employment. They have a pyramidal organization structure, just as we do for our titled positions. But because of their investment in people, their actual staffing exceeds the confines of the pyramid in the middle and upper management levels. This might seem excess baggage to the western mind. But in Japan these people are valued treasure to the organization. While our titled organization is occupied with ad hoc committees and other discursive meetings, their titled organization is working on ways to improve the system. The other resources are busy visiting customers, training younger employees, participating in the ad hoc meetings and otherwise providing the social memory needed to sustain the company. We don't have this experienced work force because of our move up or out pressures.

Organization for lifetime employment

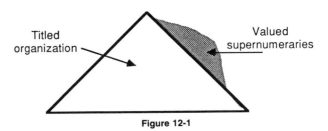

Figure 12-1

During that same trip, I was able to gain information on the extent of the education and training that goes on in the country. The cooperation of the various sectors is truly amazing. Government, industry, and academia are all involved in improving Japan's only natural resource, its people. Dr. Deming has observed:

What has Japan? Nothing except people and good management. No resources. No iron or no coal, no oil, no copper, no manganese. Not even wood for commercial purposes.[42]

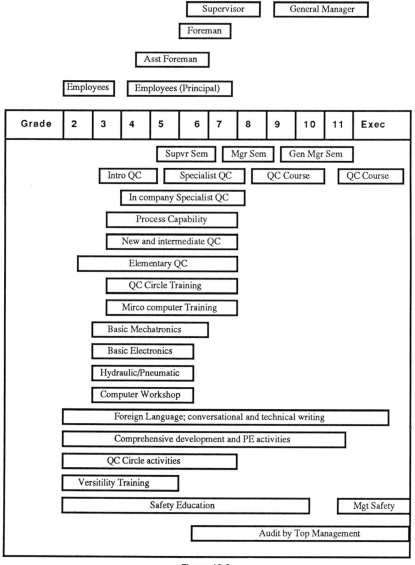

Figure 12-2

An excellent example of the commitment and cooperation involved in the development of their people comes from a Japanese steel company (Figure 12-2). There is a wide variety of courses available to their employees throughout their career. They treat it as an investment, not an expense.

A couple of years ago, I had the privilege of speaking to a group of junior and community college presidents. As I was flying to the meeting in Washington D.C., trying to figure out what I was going to say to them, I realized that they represented Ford's most important suppliers because they supplied our most important resource, our people. For years industry has accused academia of not teaching anything relevant. And for years academia has been replying that they are the bastion of theoretical purity and that industry better start using it. I think it is time for the nonacademic sectors to recognize academia as their most important supplier and either begin to work with them or develop another source.

I will make one observation about education today on which I have no solution. Industry desperately needs to foster teamwork. The only training or education on teamwork our people receive in school is on the atheletic field. Teamwork in the classroom is called cheating. We learn that in our very first day of school. Somehow we need to develop teambuilding skills in our children.

One possible approach for a stronger industry/university partnership is through the development of quality and productivity institutes, with financial support from industrial membership. The institute can provide a vehicle for which industry can present their customer needs and the university can develop improved supportive methodologies relevant to industrial problems. Additionally, the institute would aid the university in improving undergraduate and graduate programs.

The University of Tennessee and Rochester Institute of Technology, for example, already have successful programs in quality and productivity improvement. The University of Wisconsin is currently developing a quality and productivity improvement center as well.

A General Motors and University of Waterloo task force is developing an institute to serve industries in Southern Ontario. The specific objectives of this institute are the following:

i) To stimulate and encourage research in the development and implementation of statistical, probabilistic, and other quantitative methods for improving quality and productivity and managerial methods to enable transfer of technology to the workplace.

ii) To develop a seminar center which will offer courses and seminars to industry on modern statistical, probabilistic and managerial methods for improving quality and productivity, and to provide systematic follow-up of the participants to ensure the transfer of technology to the workplace.

iii) To provide a focus on campus for multidisciplinary research on statistical, probabilistic, and managerial aspects of the control and improvement of quality and productivity.

iv) To aid in the development of associated multidisciplinary undergraduate and graduate programs that will meet the growing needs of industry for engineering graduates with strong statistical backgrounds and for statistics graduates with an appreciation for the problems of engineering and manufacturing.

v) To encourage experience-exchange programs between the university faculty and personnel in industry.

vi) To encourage and stimulate research and development of alternative methods of disseminating knowledge about quality improvement in the workplace.[43]

Ford is piloting a long-term (five-year) contract with Oakland University for the development of statistical thinking in Ford's employees and the development of a real world business perspective in Oakland's faculty. Various Ford divisions have contracted with local universities to educate and reeducate their employees. For the most part, this education is on company time and at company expense (I should say at company investment). The next chapter discusses your other suppliers.

Chapter 13

End the practice of awarding business on the basis of price tag. Instead, minimize total cost. Move toward a single supplier for any one item on a long-term relationship of loyalty and trust. (Point 4)

If you are going to meet your customers' needs at a price that they are willing to pay, you must begin to establish **long-term relationships** with suppliers, encouraging them to adopt the philosophy of continuing improvement. The reason for the long-term relationships is obvious. Our suppliers can invest in the future and be secure that someone isn't going to replace them next year by underbidding on the price tag. Of course you would only want to enter into a long-term relationship with an organization that could consistently meet your needs and expectations and would improve their ability to do so over the duration of the relationship. Dr. Deming states that when you try to find an organization that meets this criterion, you will be lucky to find even one. Don't worry about finding more than one. If you follow this criterion, however, the number of multiple source items will dramatically decrease along with the associated high costs of this waste.

The above words are easy to say and, in fact, many people think that this is one of the easiest of the principles to implement. It just takes top management to decree longer-term contracts and no more than one supplier per part. In reality, the change can be much harder to implement, especially if top management has not provided the road map.

In 1983, Mr. L.M. Chicoine, Ford's Vice President for Purchasing and Supply, was convinced that what Dr. Deming said about long-term contracts was the way Ford should conduct its business. He was in the process of a long series of discussions with some of his important customers, executives from Ford's supply base. They told him that long-term relationships would benefit everyone. Then, with a mandate from Mr. Petersen to improve relations with and results from the supply base, he issued the statement that he would like to see an increasing number of long-term contracts. (At Ford, a long-term contract was essentially any contract with a period of performance greater than one year.) After about six months, he received a status report on the number of long-term contracts, and it hadn't really increased. It had not increased in large part because there was a procedure that said that a buyer must submit for approval, through two levels of supervision, any contract written for *greater* than one year. So in spite his vision, in spite of his good intent, not much had happened because very few buyers were willing to go through the hassle of two layers of supervision with all the required justification, just to get some supplier a long-term contract. He quickly saw to it that this procedure was changed. A change of one word resulted in the rapid increase in the number of long-term contracts. Now if a buyer wants to write a contract for *less* than one year, he must get two levels of supervisory approval! What is important to note here is that no improvement could be made until management changed the system, specifically the method or procedure that guided other people's actions.

We should choose suppliers based on quality of product and services as well as cost. Suppliers should be able to provide evidence of sustained statistical control. This implies that buyers should be trained in ways to interpret the evidence of sustained statistical control. I have seen one enterprising supplier submit a sequence of control charts in which the control limits appeared closer and closer together. This is normally a positive sign of variability reduction and higher quality if the right target is being met. The semitrained buyer was estatic when he saw this; his supplier was showing continuing improvement. Only upon closer examination did he realize the supplier had taken the same control chart and reduced it in a copier machine! I guess some of the "experts" are right; you do not need

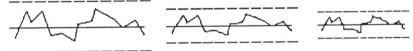

Figure 13-1

extensive training to show continuing improvement.

The misuse or confusion between the customer and the process feedback loops results in waste. Understanding their signals, however, results in satisfied customers, employees, and suppliers. Both the supplier and the customer can misuse the information.

For instance, if I am a customer who makes a one-time purchase, as Dr. Deming describes in Chapter 2 of *Out of the Crisis,* then I can make my choice independent of what the supplier's process will generate next. By buying the outcome, I am signalling to the supplier, through the customer feedback loop, that this is my number one choice. I have that perogative as a customer. I can see the difference between the various outcomes offered to me, and I select the one that is best suited for my use.

The supplier, however, had better not change or reblend his process inputs based solely upon my (the customer's) feedback. Before he reblends his incoming resources, he must listen to his process performance through his process feedback loop. If he adjusts his process based upon my feedback, whether it be praise or complaint, he runs the risk of overcontrol and its associated losses.

Now, if the customer wants to buy a number of items over time, then he must not make the decision independent of the process information. Thus, Dr. Deming's advice for the customer is to require statistical evidence from the supplier's process feedback loop. In this situation, the customer is buying not only the outcomes, but also the process that produces them.

In order to consistently meet our customers' needs, we need to limit the number of suppliers for any single part to just one. We know that administrative costs will decrease, but the big savings accrue with reduced variability, as we saw in Chapter 4. Even though different suppliers deliver parts within the specifications, they are not the same. In fact, even the same supplier but different shipping points contribute to greater variability than a single shipping point.

Three very good suppliers combine to produce a mediocre result

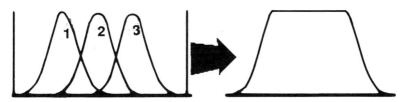

Figure 13-2

This principle applies to any supplier, not just to the obvious over-the-fence supplier. In-house suppliers are affected as well. Each of us is a supplier to another process. The order processing and invoicing department is a supplier to accounts receivable, design is a supplier to engineering, operation 10 is a supplier to operation 20. Historically, the first commandment of manufacturing has been thou shalt not shut down the production line. We install parallel machines so that if one goes down, others can feed and be fed by yet several others. This is just another example of suboptimization. You might be better able to reduce your total cost if you aimed at the output of a series of supplier/customer processes and did not reroute the output. In the simple example below, there are 18 possible paths that could take place if you use the method of routing around trouble spots to keep production running.

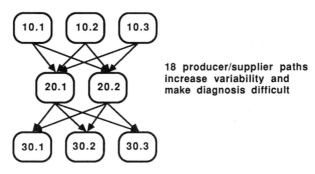

Figure 13-3

If you targeted the output of the processes to match the figure there would only be 4 paths. This method reduces the cost of time and money in troubleshooting problems. It also results in less variability as seen by the ultimate customer, because adjusting the mean is easier than adjusting other sources of variability.

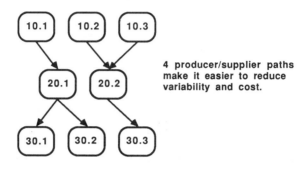

4 producer/supplier paths make it easier to reduce variability and cost.

Figure 13-4

Another process which can be affected by the number of suppliers is the process of assisting your outside suppliers to improve their quality. Ford calls these people Supplier Quality Assistance or SQA for short. In 1983, there were 1194 outside supplier locations which had more than one SQA activity supplying them with assistance. In fact, one supplier location had people from seven SQA activities giving direction.

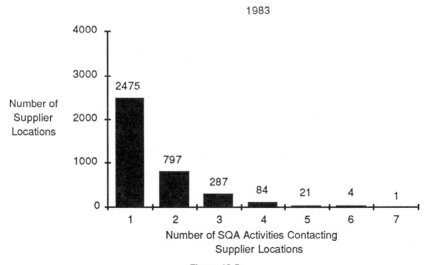

Figure 13-5

The costs due to conflicting direction, administration, and redundancy are obvious. In a little under two years, the number and the distribution has changed dramatically. In 1984, no supplier location had over three SQA activities visiting them.

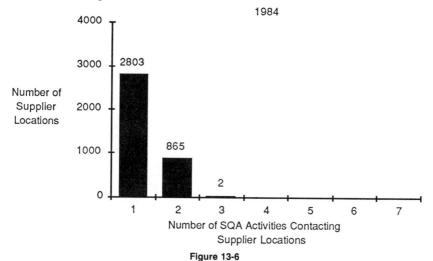

Figure 13-6

It took the concerted efforts of a team of people not only from SQA but purchasing and engineering and our suppliers. In 1985, the number of supplier locations having even two SQA activities assisting them was reduced to 120.

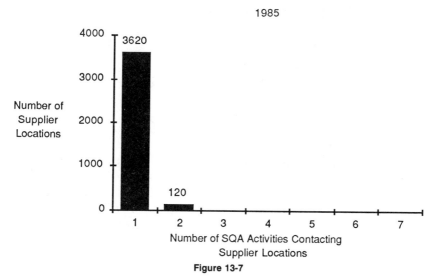

Figure 13-7

It may be that the 120 supplier locations that have two SQA activities are an irreducible minimum. But chances are that it is not. And under the philosophy of continuing improvement, Ford is looking for ways to reduce it even further so that they might better assist their outside suppliers.[44]

Chapter 14

Put everybody in the organization to work to accomplish the transformation. The transformation is everybody's job. (Point 14)

This is the difficult one, both to explain and to do. It is difficult because I don't think there is any theory to guide us. What worked in one organization might not work in another. We are all managing processes with different and changing inputs. Dr. Deming has a very definite recommendation on organization for the transformation. His recommendation is based on experience and the observation that this proposal comes out far ahead of other approaches.

It is one thing to have a dotted line relationship on paper, quite another thing to have it in reality. I have found that the dotted line can make a better transition to becoming a reality with the assignment of statisticians to key operating vice presidents and general managers. These statisticians are their senior manager's alter ego. They sit in on their operating review meetings, tutor them in statistical thinking and Dr. Deming's philosophy, identify inhibiting management systems, and coordinate action on opportunities for improvement. Not every statistician can handle this assignment. Dr. Deming has stated that these people must have the following characteristics:

• Attainment of a master's level in mathematics and statistical theory, preferably beyond this level, and with continuing education.

• Experience of five years or more in government or industry on production, design, measurement systems, standardization of tests, testing in the laboratory, testing in the field, interlaboratory testing, or other experience.

• Possessed of a burning desire to be effective in industry.

• Ability to work with management on sources of improvement of processes, methods, and style of management.

• Be a good listener, to understand problems and other people's perception about what the problem is and what to do.

• Be a good team man, yet unwilling to compromise, unwilling to settle for less than what appears to him to be optimum practice under the circumstances.

• Modesty and built-in good manners, able to associate with and work with people in top positions as an equal, not as superior or inferior. Likewise with engineers, sales, and hourly workers. In my experience, some candidates need to attend a finishing school for a year.

• Ability to teach the philosophy in Deming's book in management, engineering, purchasing, personnel, law, etc., to these same people. A statistician must have attended Deming's four-day seminar. He must have the ability to teach statistical thinking and methods.[45]

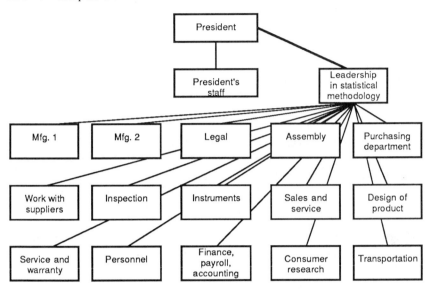

ORGANIZATION FOR QUALITY

Figure 14-1

Some general managers from manufacturing organizations immediately recognized the benefits of the personal statistician. Others in financial and administrative organizations took a while longer. Still others remain to be convinced of the need. No statistician should be assigned to a general manager until that manager really wants the help. In the meantime, the leader of statistical methodology must help his customers (the senior management of the organization) recognize that their needs include this help. I have found this approach more conducive to reinforcing the fact that quality is a line responsibility, not a staff responsibility. There should be no need to build a large staff organization. We are uncompetitive enough in our overhead structure. I advocate a matrix of responsibilities for this small staff organization. Each statistician should have organizational as well as functional responsibilities, the intent being to cover and help along the many complex interrelationship combinations that can occur in an organization. For example, the statistician assigned to a regional organization might also have responsibility for the engineering function in the entire organization. Other identifiable functions include finance, administration, manufacturing, etc.

He will meet his regional organization's needs by arranging help from other functional experts. He himself will help other regions with his expertise in engineering applications of statistical methods.

Skills in leadership, not just skills in management, must predominate as an organization makes the transition to continuing improvement. I don't think there is a member of top management anywhere who doesn't sincerely believe that he is for quality. Now they all have their own definition of it, but they are all for it. The problem is to move that sincerity from the wishes and hopes category to reality. To some, quality is profits; to others, quality is meeting customers' needs. To yet others, quality is staying in business, or meeting schedules, or being bought out, or being number one in market share. Whatever their vision, they must carry it out. You notice that I did not say that they should see that it is carried out because you cannot delegate responsibility.

Many times that vision is short-circuited by middle management. Now, I am not blaming middle management; they are doing what they think top managment wants, or at least what they saw top management do when they were middle management. It is not easy to identify this absorbing layer of management. They restrict the flow of information in all directions. They have seen programs come and go, and can wait out almost any change. They can do this because they know that their management is only looking at what they accomplish, at their outcomes. If senior management is going to get the message through this layer of middle management, they must break with tradition that says "Do not tell managers how to do something, just tell them what you want done." The supposition is that management is experienced enough to figure out how to accomplish the outcome. Today's manager would be insulted if his boss discussed how he wanted something done. After all, the manager is senior enough and responsible enough to figure out how to do it. He just wants to be given an assignment and the latitude to carry it out. The problem with this approach is that it focuses on the outcomes and not on the process which produces them. The problem is compounded by the fact that this approach is used too far down in the organization. Everyone delegates. Everyone nods agreement. Nothing changes. Sometimes this not discussing the "how" is very purposively avoided. How many times have you heard in a crisis, "I don't want to know how you get it done, that's your problem. Just do it." If management is to improve their organization, they must change the process. This means that they cannot accept conference room promises, but must work directly with their people on the process, the how and the why. During this period of transition, everyone must be willing to learn. There is no room for fear of learning. No one is too senior to be involved in the how.

As organizations proceed to implement Dr. Deming's philosophy, they sometimes plateau at a particular quality level. At the very least, the rate of improvement is not as great as it was in the beginning of their efforts. There are varying reasons for this, including some of the false starts that Dr. Deming has observed. But much of the plateauing is attributed to management not living up to their responsibilities to change the processes that they are responsible for. I draw an analogy to the energy crisis, when you could save some good amounts of energy just by some simple actions of turning off the lights and the thermostat up or down a few degrees, depending on the season. You can get better quality initially by just paying attention to what you are doing, or working a bit harder, if you will. You can get even more improvement by working a bit smarter, too. But without system change, the learning curve predictably levels off.

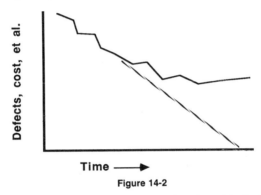

Figure 14-2

It is in this period that management action is critical. The organization needs them to act as leaders more than ever before. But it is in this period that managers are tempted to resort to platitudes of working harder in the system in hopes of following the curve of their initial progress (dashed line). What can you do to avoid this plateauing? There is no simple or universal answer. I use a three-pronged approach to implement Dr. Deming's philosophy. There is no underlying theory to support this, but it met with some success at Ford.

● You must see to it that everyone in the organization, supply base, and distribution network is trained in ways to continually improve. This training, as you saw in Chapters 11 and 12, is more than just statistics. But as you also saw, training is not enough.

● You must improve or remove management systems which stand in the way of continuing improvement.

● You must identify and take action on opportunities to improve at every level. These success stories can help spread the institutionalization of the philosophy. Action shows you are serious. Rhetoric shows nothing has changed.

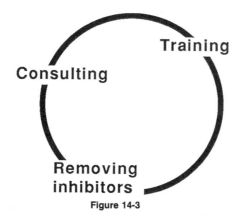

Figure 14-3

Training senior management can be extremely difficult because of their superstitious learning. Many will not learn in a classroom environment. There is too much fear of knowledge. The manager will hesitate to ask candid questions because it might show weakness, and his people will not ask the questions because "if the manager and the others understood it, I am not going to look dumb". Thus the statistician must tutor the manager in Dr. Deming's philosophy, but especially in statistical methods. The senior manager will have knowledge of different subject matters and the statistician must not be presumptuous in those matters.

The statistician must review all training in the organization for consistency in statistical thinking. He must not be caught in the trap of being the person who requests managers to send people to the training. I have found that it can be very easy for the "statistical coordinator" to request a plant manger to send ten people to a course. No muss, no fuss. This is not the statistician's job. It is the job of the plant manager's boss. The chain of command must be actively involved in this process; otherwise, people will look to the staff for training and guidance and not to their boss. In fact, the training should not only be requested by their boss but also actively involve their boss as I described in Chapter 11. I have also found that just-in-time training is needed when you teach skills and tools to adults. Unless they have an opportunity to use the skills or tools within a few weeks, they will lose them. All that remain are the buzzwords. That is why I advocate splitting your time between training and consulting. Unless you can follow up the training with an actual application, you are probably not as effective as you could be.

Removing inhibitors requires that the statistician coach his senior manager on asking questions which are consistent with Dr. Deming's philosophy. The statistician must review Chapter 5, "Questions to Help Managers" from Dr. Deming's *Out of the Crisis*.[2] Another source of questions that I would recommend only for the more advanced, comes from the checklist used by

JUSE to evaluate companies challenging for the Deming Prize. There are ten major categories of questions:

- Policy
- Organization and Management
- Education and Dissemination
- Information Accumulation and Utilization System
- Analysis
- Standardization
- Control
- Quality Assurance
- Effectiveness
- Future Planning

What follows are some of the questions I ask to determine understanding and execution of the Fourteen Points.

Point 1.

Has the Board of Directors attended a Deming seminar?

Have all senior management and high potential people attended a Deming seminar?

Has the "critical mass" of people attended a Deming seminar?

Has the organization published/disseminated its mission?

How do you know it was understood?

Has management committed to attrition for reduced personnel requirements?

What process do you have to determine customer needs?

What process do you have to improve consistency of purpose?

What have you done to ensure that consistency of purpose will remain after you are gone?

Point 2.

Do you know what it takes to get your customer to brag?

Do you know the loss incurred by not meeting your customers' needs?

Is this new philosophy part of your training at all levels?

Point 3.

Where do you rely on mass inspection?

What are you doing to eliminate it?

Operationally define continuing improvement.

Show me an example of it in a process that you manage.

How do you know that you are improving to meet your customers' needs for now and for three years hence?

Point 4.

Have purchasing, manufacturing, and engineering departments a common set of goals?

Is purchasing charged with the cost of inspecting the incoming resource before it is used? They should be.

How many single-source suppliers have you?
Is that greater than last period?
Operationally define long term.
How many long-term relationships with suppliers do you have?
Is that more than last period?
Point 5.
Show me the Deming Cycle in action on a process that you manage.
Point 6.
What systems that would curtail the effectiveness of training have you changed for the better?
Is training part of everyone's objectives?
How do you know when training is no longer effective?
Point 7.
How much time do you spend managing people rather than outcomes?
If you manage by exception, how do you define it?
What are your criteria for giving feedback?
What barriers have you removed which inhibited your people from improving?
Point 8.
Do you feel that your boss propagates fear?
Do your subordinates fear you? How do you know?
What steps are you taking to reduce fear?
Point 9.
Who are the people outside your immediate organization on teams established by you to help you on your processes?
Point 10.
What do your people consider meaningless slogans?
How do you know?
Point 11.
How do you know that you have put in a full day's work?
How do you measure work output for administrative processes?
Where are the places your organization uses work standards?
What is your plan to eliminate them?
What targets have you?
How did you arrive at them?
Are they point estimates or ranges?
What is the process by which you will reach your target?
Point 12.
Have you surveyed your organization to identify barriers to continuing improvement?
What are they?
What are you doing about them?
Do you feel that you can honestly and openly communicate with your boss?

Point 13.

What training have you attended these past twelve months?

What have you done to personally train your people?

What should your people know ten years from now?

What are your plans to make sure they do?

Point 14.

What have you done to signal that it is not business as usual?

What are you doing to learn more about statistical thinking?

Who in middle management can thwart this effort by stonewalling, conference room promises, or open rejection? What are you doing about it?

How often do you discuss the Fourteen Points with your subordinates? Peers? Superiors?

To whom do you go for statistical advice?

What was the most recent advice?

You convey your priorities by your questions and actions, not by your intentions. In this period of transition, you must, at the very least, make it clear that you are willing to unfreeze management systems. You must be willing to consider that there are some things that you and your people do today that you cannot be doing tomorrow. Management has a history of adding on programs to an already full plate. As we lose people by attrition, we cannot expect those who remain to be burdened by the inhibitors of today.

Consulting and taking action gets the theory out of the classroom and into the real world. Many people still take a Thomasian view of wanting to touch and feel in order to believe. One man in Ford's Plastic Paint and Vinyl Division said in a folksy way, "Spray some paint on it so I can see it." Case studies in nonmanufacturing applications are especially useful because one, these areas do not have a recognized history of using quality discipline and two, the vast majority of opportunities for improvement are in the nonmanufacturing area. Obviously, most of management are involved in nonmanufacturing processes. As I said back in Chapter 5, management needs to learn about variability and then begin to apply that new knowledge to processes that they manage. It is very important to demonstrate your leadership by initiating a case study on one of your processes. It could be as personal and simple as reviewing what you spend your time on, or as leveraged and complex as changing a companywide management system.

Getting started is difficult. If you are not the top person in your organization, then you must be concerned about how to get your boss involved. Just like any other customer, you must know his needs and expectations in order to get him involved. There is no universally applicable plan for this task. Some top managers view themselves as without peer in the organization; others take counsel from a set of trusted advisors. Some will only listen to an outside expert, others only if it is their idea. It is fashionable nowadays to listen to employee involvement or quality of worklife groups, especially salaried groups. Some in management are looking for opportunities to respond to some meaningful employee initiatives; others will never change. There is no substitute for knowledge here. Just as much as your boss should understand your needs as a person/customer, so should you understand your boss' needs as a person/customer.

Fear of change might be mitigated by talking to others who are going on many of the same roads as you are. Dr. Deming has urged this comiseration/communication for decades.

> One thing you can do - that is very necessary for you to do - is to have meetings with each other wherever it is possible. These meetings and the groups that meet need not be at all formal; they can be very simply organized. All you need is someone willing to make the arrangements: find a speaker, notify the members of the group and fix some place. In most cities, there can usually be found a professor who... could assist you considerably. This afternoon I suggest you meet together and discuss what could be done, and decide. The main thing is to do something quickly. After two or three years, you will look back on this year 1950, and you will be able to see the result. At first many discouraging things may happen and you may be disappointed. You will have to be patient ... you must never let your studies stop. I believe that the power that started here will become a great asset for Japan - a power for better living, for happier living, for peace, and for the good of the world. ₁

In recent years, Deming User Groups (DUG's) have formed in various parts of the world. The nation of New Zealand, the state of Wisconsin, the region around Lawrence, Massachusetts, the county of Orange in California, the city of Philadelphia, the Chamber of Commerce in Spartanburg, South Carolina, a group of businessmen in Amsterdam, are but a few of the locations and types of these groups. Each of them has one thing in common — a desire to better understand and implement the philosophy of Dr. Deming. One DUG in particular has been proactive in its efforts to spread the philosophy. That group is the San Diego DUG, under the careful coordination of Dr. Laurie Broedling. The American Quality and Productivity Institute, under the guidance of Dr. Myron Tribus, is a growing source of information on the Deming Philosophy. AQPI has a computerized bulletin board and sponsors conferences on the Deming Philosophy. The list is growing daily.

REFERENCES

1. DEMING, W. EDWARDS. *Elementary Principles of the Statistical Control of Quality.* Nippon Kagaku Gijutsu Remmei JUSE, 1951.

2. DEMING, W. EDWARDS. *Quality, Productivity, and Competitive Position* or *Out of the Crisis.* MIT Center for Advanced Engineering Study, 1982.

3. *U. S. News & World Report,* p.64, 10 Oct 83.

4. DRUCKER, PETER F. *Forbes,* p.128, 23 May 83.

5. *Business Week,* p.86, 13 Aug 84.

6. OUCHI, WILLIAM G. *The M-Form Society.* Addison-Wesley, 1984, p. 31.

7. Ibid., p. 56.

8. DRUCKER, PETER F. *Forbes,* p. 125, 23 May 83.

9. TRIBUS, MYRON. *Productivity Brief* Number 33. American Productivity Center, 1984.

10. OUCHI, WILLIAM G. *The M-Form Society.* Addison-Wesley, 1984, p. 4.

11. PETERSEN, D.E. *Opening Remarks at a 3-day Dr. Deming Statistical Seminar.* February 10-12, 1982.

12. BAKER, E.M. and ARTINIAN, H.L.M. "The Deming Philosophy of Continuing Improvement in a Service Organization: The Case of Windsor Export Supply". *Quality Progress,* June 1985.

13. SCHWINN, DAVID R. *Transformation of American Industry.* QIP Inc., 1984.

14. WIGGER, J. Ford of Europe, 1984.

15. *Continuing Process Control and Process Capability Improvement.* Ford Motor Company, 1984. Chapter 1.

16. *Car and Driver* p.33, Aug 83.

17. SCHERKENBACH, W. and SIEGEL, J. "Recent Statistical Applications", Society of Manufacturing Engineers Tool and Manufacturing Engineering Conference, May 1983.

18. JESSUP, PETER T. "Process Capability, The Value of Improved Performance", 24 June 85. Proceedings of ICC 85, Institute of Electrical and Electronics Engineers.

19. OUCHI, WILLIAM G. *The M-Form Society.* Addison-Wesley, 1984, p. 35.

20. SAUNDERS, DAVID M. Private communication with W. Scherkenbach, 1985.

21. *Wall Street Journal,* 14 Sep 81.

22. *The San Diego Union,* 21 Feb 83, C2.

23. *Dun's Business Month,* Oct 84, p.57.

24. KANTER, ROSABETH MOSS. *The Change Masters.* Simon and Shuster, 1983, p85.

25. *Detroit News,* September 28, 1982, 1A.

26. IACOCCA, LEE. *Iacocca An Autobiography.* Bantam, 1984, Chapter 5.

27. *Business Week,* 2 Apr 84.

28. *Business Week,* 13 Aug 84, p.88.

29. CLAUSING, DON P. "Product Development Process, Overview and Needs". 1985.

30. Ford Motor Company, "Design Approval Process Improvement Project", January 1984.

31. *Automotive Industries,* Jan 85, p.23.

32. CHAMBERS, DAVID S. Private communication with W. Scherkenbach, 1982.

33. DEMING, W. EDWARDS. Private communication with W. Scherkenbach, 1984.

34. LEWIS, C.I. *Mind and the World Order.* Dover Publications, 1956.

35. KILMANN, RALPH H. *Beyond the Quick Fix.* Jossey-Bass, 1984, p. x.

36. Nashua Conference--Excerpts from a presentation by William Conway to Ford Executives, 1981.

37. DEMING, W. EDWARDS. "Boundaries of Statistical Inference," Chapter 31. Johnson, N. L. and Smith, H. *New Developments in Survey Sampling.* John Wiley, 1969.

38. DEMING, W. EDWARDS. *Some Theory of Sampling.* Dover, 1950, p. vii.

39. TUKEY, J.W. *Exploratory Data Analysis.* Addison Wesley, 1977.

40. TAGUCHI, GENICHI AND WU, YU-IN. *Introduction To Off-Line Quality Control.* Central Japan Quality Control Association.

41. DEMING, W. EDWARDS. Conversation with W. Scherkenbach, 1984.

42. DEMING, W. EDWARDS. Speech to Automotive Division ASQC, 4 Nov 83.

43. MOEN, RON. Private communication with W. Scherkenbach, 1986.

44. Ford Corporate Quality Office data, 1985.

45. DEMING, W. EDWARDS. Private communication, 12 January 1985.

46. GARFIELD, CHARLES. *Peak Performers.* William Morrow and Company, Inc., 1986, p. 236.

INDEX